supporting publishing journey! I hope you enjoy my book! Wishing you a happy, healthy and successful 2025!

THE VINTAGE MINDSET

all my best,

Jillian

THE VINTAGE MINDSET

JILLIAN MCCARTHY

NEW DEGREE PRESS

THE VINTAGE MINDSET

ISBN   978-1-63676-571-6   *Paperback*

          978-1-63676-170-1   *Kindle Ebook*

          978-1-63676-172-5   *Ebook*

This book is dedicated to my many wonderful teachers at Medford High School, in particular, Mr. Ambrose, Mr. Milne, and Ms. Daneau. Thank you for inspiring me each and every day.

CONTENTS

———

*"Don't buy much, but make sure
that what you buy is good."*

- CHRISTIAN DIOR

PREFACE

The history of fashion thus far can be characterized by materialism, over-consumption, and irresponsible business practices. However, the devastating results of the global health pandemic caused by COVID-19 have put the effects of such practices and the outrageous consumer demand for instant gratification into the spotlight. In the near future, brands will face polarizing views regarding the state of fashion and the future of an entire industry based on consumer demand for discounted, low priced, and frequently updated items. I predict that consumer values will soon shift to place a pressing importance on sustainability, which will give brands a critical opportunity to reinvent themselves within the new, emerging landscape.

The fashion industry—particularly that of fast fashion[1]—is highly pollutive of the environment and uses many questionable sourcing and production methods to meet consumers'

---

1   Fast fashion refers to a business model within the industry in which many companies profit off of copying couture straight from the runway and replicating it at low-cost for the masses.

demands and keep costs low. The industry's increasingly environmentally destructive and morally unethical processes are not solely the fault of consumer demand—many people are unaware since this information is not readily available for a consumer. To make matters more complicated, most consumers are not fashion experts; even if they seek out information, they will likely not be able to understand the effects of textile costs on pricing or be attuned to the differences in processes behind artisan leather produced at a small farm in Tuscany for a luxury label versus faux leather containing toxic chemicals produced in India for a fast fashion retailer whose name they recognize. As the fast fashion model increased in popularity, so did the number of brands and businesses that replicated or mimicked luxury goods at affordable prices and much lower quality than real thing.

The necessary changes to the fashion industry will not happen overnight, but we have reached a point where we can now fathom how unnecessary our fashion consumption is. We have reached a tipping point and we are all aware the industry we love that fosters our imagination and drives our creativity cannot go back to the way it was before the pandemic.

As the world hesitantly enters 2021, we see political uncertainty, dangerous climate change, and a rapidly evolving digital landscape, to everyone's great dismay. Due to these changes, people have developed a newfound sense of urgency to diminish their carbon footprint; this growing emphasis on sustainability has created a market crowded with eco-friendly

---

Chloe Foussianes, "What Is Fast Fashion, and Why Is Everyone Talking About It?," Town & Country, January 17, 2020.

brands that are actually 'greenwashing'—or falsely advertising—how the companies actually produce their products and relay information about their brand as a whole.

Through all of the uncertainty behind a sustainable ethos such as regard for factory garment workers, environmental impact, and natural textiles and fibers, there are some key players who are actually changing the landscape as fashion as we know it. Independent innovators, dreamers, and promoters of the future of fashion follow closely behind these key players.

Sustainable brands like Patagonia, Stella McCartney, Eileen Fisher, Mara Hoffman, and other smaller labels are the current talk of the fashion industry; however, these brands are unable to effectively reach the masses for a number of reasons, such as price point, brand positioning, and physical retail location to customer segmentation and targeting. If there are not enough brands that can effectively appeal to and convince the everyday consumer to purchase their sustainable products, how else can the industry and our planet as a whole have a future? The answer lies in the past.

Think about the gorgeous pair of creamy white trousers from the '90s hanging in your closet. Or the raggedy but beloved '80s Queen band tee folded in your drawer. What do these two items have in common? Not only were they both dug out of a vintage store somewhere, but they also brought a thrill to the retail experience when you the discovered something unexpected from the past. Fashion consumers love the idea of going into a store to find something they do not need but rather something that excites and satisfies their need to consume.

The retail landscape has shifted dramatically with the rise of technology in the digital age. People can order groceries to their door on their lunch break with their smartphone. Retailers have shuttered their doors and revamped their online presence. Institutions such as Barneys New York and various concept stores from Colette to Opening Ceremony have been acquired and shut down. Specialty stores across the country such as Louis of Boston have disappeared. The thrill of retail no longer rests in the suburban shopping mall; consumers order via Amazon Prime and find products they once saw in stores marked down by 30 percent online.

Despite the shift to online shopping over the past several years, there are still two places consumers can visit to seek a new and interesting experience: vintage stores and off-price retailers. Both of these types of stores provide the opportunity for customers to find something new and unexpected, whether they really need it or not. The idea of walking into a store and having no idea what you might find is distinctly rare in a society that quite literally runs on services that bring us exactly what we want, when we want it.

The idea of buying vintage pieces has two distinct effects on consumers. Some consumers—specifically the younger generational cohorts of Millennial and Gen Z-ers—thoroughly enjoy shopping vintage to enjoy a nostalgic past that is essentially inaccessible today. In contrast, another group of consumers refuses to shop vintage because they view the second-hand market as unsophisticated and outdated. This viewpoint is concerning when you consider the tremendous benefit that shopping vintage has on the fashion industry; it is the most sustainable version of consumption. In this context, the term, 'sustainable,' means that buying used clothing is a way of extending the life of a retail item, whether it be a pair of beloved leather Gucci loafers or a retro 1980s ski jacket. Shopping vintage prolongs the time consumers use a garment, therefore testing its quality and flaunting its age rather than keeping it for a season and tossing it out as it goes out of style.

The prolonging and increased utility of a garment has inspired Marist College senior and fashion design student, Isabel Holden, to design her final capsule collection around sustainability and natural dying techniques. Holden is somewhat of a trailblazer in the Gen Z design community, recently winning the prestigious undergraduate Council of Fashion Designers of America's (CFDA) Liz Claiborne Design Scholarship Award in 2019. Holden won the award for her commitment to cross-discipline and environmentally conscious design work, which she displayed in her senior design collection presented at Marist's Silver Needle Runway show in May 2020.

What is perhaps the greatest takeaway from Holden's successes is her motivation to fix the wasteful consumption habits of fashion, which she spearheads in a collaborative manner. Dame Ellen MacArthur, founder of the Ellen MacArthur Foundation that focuses on bringing the idea of a circular economy to scale, names collaborating as one of her four major points to successfully implement the concept of circularity. In fact, industry professionals, designers, and innovators alone cannot carry out every single idea for reinventing, restructuring, and restoring the fashion industry; the new age of the fashion industry must be a collaborative vision with consumers as well.

Despite the growing awareness around fast fashion and its implications—the mass production of low-quality, inexpensive goods copied and replicated directly from the latest runway trends—there are still milestones to reach to help eradicate the extensive human and environmental costs that have been completely exposed due to the global pandemic. The alternative we must consciously choose now is the idea of 'slow fashion,' which involves ethical labor standards, sustainable sourcing methods, and the production of high-quality garments made to last. As fashion students, industry professionals, and young creatives, we must make the choice to not only make the world a more beautiful place but also to make it a healthier one.

'Green' fashion has failed the industry considerably due to lack of funding, innovation, poor reporting, and an overall consensus to prioritize profit over environmental standards. Consumers are confused, and moreover, skeptical of the 'sustainable' practices that companies claim to use. This skeptical mindset is perhaps the largest barrier that brands face moving forward, for they have dug themselves into a deep hole that will take not only a lot of willpower to escape, but also new methodologies and a determination to win over consumers. In this new era, brands have the opportunity to carry out new consumer values of quality, ethical practices, and craftsmanship. Companies can now align themselves with these values instead of the previous values of constant newness, discounts, and inferior quality. In doing so, brands can also create an inclusive community for its consumers, which will foster an authentic environment and, in turn, brand loyalty.

Loyalty is the most crucial element of any brand and is difficult to find with shoppers in a crowded marketplace filled with different ideas, products, and values. Word of mouth marketing from loyal consumers is incredibly powerful, and even more so when it comes naturally from the brand's personal community of shoppers rather than from paying outside celebrities and influencers to advertise their brand message.

If brands begin to cultivate an inclusive community, they can participate in the circular model of clothing as well; brands can actually foster programs in which consumers sell clothing back to the original retailer and it becomes part of a new line. Major brands that are already grounded in a sustainable ethos, such as Eileen Fisher and Stella McCartney, have put frameworks in place to foster this kind of renewal program.

The power of the vintage mindset lies in convincing consumers that they are not just buying a second-hand item, but rather, they are renewing an item, giving another life to its former story, and carrying it into the future. However, the language is important; consumers must have a 'vintage' mindset rather than the notion of 'second-hand.' The lack of success in the vintage market taking off is in part due to the negative connotations with owning something that someone else has already used. Other challenges that the vintage market faces have to do with the effort from consumers; there is work behind the hunt, intimidation of trying to find something interesting and cool, and plenty of uncertainty about why to actually purchase. To combat these challenges, there is a wide range of options for brands to pick up on.

For example, brands could start to foster their own renewal lines that encourage the return of an old product from any time period, invest in repairing and reworking the item, and resell it as its own individual line in a cool concept store that draws consumer attention. Young fashion students and older, more stylish career-driven fashionistas could also set up social platforms or online shops specially curated with vintage items or create guides to shopping vintage. Although most of the vintage mindset is innate, all it takes is accumulating the knowledge of brands, product, time periods, and locations in which you could possibly find these goods. Then it is up to the individual consumer to frequent these shops and foster relationships with the sales personnel. This shift in mindset is vital to convincing more consumers to shop vintage and also to encourage the circular economy, which will encourage higher-quality products with longer life spans than those products distributed by mass fashion retailers.

As a fashion merchandising student, I have sat through numerous design meetings, handled hundreds of samples, and catalogued such samples and swatches, all while a nagging voice in my head questioned everything I was doing. That voice asked me, "Why do we need all these samples? Can't we utilize a digital model to swap and adjust styles?"

I wrote this book for the young people who are revolutionizing the way we shop and interact with fashion. I will discuss such topics such as:

- the current state of fashion through the eyes of a fashion student
- alternative fashion business structures to make our industry more sustainable
- interviews with industry professionals and an innovative, award-winning student fashion designer

I have always been the black sheep of my generation, actually falling on the cusp of Gen Z-ers and Millennials. While I do prefer physical books and papers to online ones, I also enjoy technology. I love that I can get my daily briefings sent to my email and flick through Vogue Runway on an iPad, but if everyday life can become increasingly digital, why am I not seeing those changes implemented in multimillion-dollar corporate fashion companies? Why are brands not investing in these energy saving, material saving, and cost saving technologies? I know there has to be a better way to continue to manufacture beautiful things, but these products need to become items that last. We—global consumers as a whole—need to come together. There must be a drastic shift within our mindset of consumption. My mother grew up wearing her sister's clothes then passing them onto her cousin. What happened to apparel that can withstand 20+ years of wear (with some minor patches)?

My summers spent as a women's merchandising intern in New York City has taught me many things. They have opened my eyes to everything from archaic and inhibitive design and merchandising processes to new design and innovation. Most importantly, these summers have made me question whether I really want to spend my life in an industry in which more than half of fast fashion product is disposed of within less than a year and where less than one percent of textiles created to make clothing is recycled into new clothing. Despite the start of a new decade, there have been so few initiatives that attempt to change these statistics on a wider scale.

I know, however, that passion and ambition can drive these changes and that truly collaborative efforts cannot only strategize change but can implement it.

CHAPTER 1

THE NEW FASHION LANDSCAPE

SUMMARY

The nature of fashion has suddenly and dramatically shifted due to the disruption caused by COVID-19. Observers have long demanded changes of the fashion industry, as it is the second most environmentally polluting industry just after the oil and gas sector. With an unclear future ahead of us, we will see a true shift in digital platforms, seasonless designs, and an overall decline of the wholesale model while DTC (direct-to-consumer) brands surge.[2] The entire industry can utilize this disruption to reshape the landscape of global supply chains and changing consumer demands.

Now it is more important than ever to use digital media strategies to create inclusive brand identities that resonate with global consumers, especially younger consumers who

---

2   Lidewij 'Li' Edelkoort, "Special Edition: Inside Fashion," March 27, 2020, in *The Business of Fashion Podcast*, produced by BoF, podcast, MP3 audio.

are quickly becoming the largest spenders. The consumer lifestyle has shifted completely in the digital age, and the direct results of COVID-19 have exacerbated the need for total change, not only in the fashion industry but also within wellness, beauty, education, restaurants, and more. Brands must now demonstrate their generosity and show solidarity with their consumer base. Since this pandemic affects everyone, it is important not to remain aloof to a worldwide crisis that has deteriorated supply chain operations and disrupted the labor and stock markets.

Brands remaining aloof during these trying times have shown the world just how tone deaf they really are; for example, Chanel debuted their Cruise Collection in the brand's first digital fashion show in the midst of massive Black Lives Matter movements and protests across the United States. In contrast, Rag & Bone released a heartfelt digital letter about the turbulent times we find ourselves in from its founder, Marcus Wainwright, in the beginning of the pandemic, marked all of its merchandise down, and is continuing its markdowns into the fall.[3] These two brands displayed their imposing differences with these actions; while Chanel had a digital couture fashion show at the height of political and civil unrest in the middle of a global pandemic, Rag & Bone released an honest letter from the brand's founder that addresses the difficulty of navigating a pandemic which directly questioned the excessive buying habits of consumers and made people think about what they actually need.

---

3   Marcus Wainwright, "A Message From Our Founder," Rag & Bone New York, accessed in March 2020.

The only way for a brand to successfully emerge from this pandemic is by fostering a sense of community through conversations that allow everyone's voice to be heard. During this time, brands cannot be 'tone deaf' to this situation and focus on profit. Sales are down across all sectors from apparel and footwear to luxury goods and e-commerce as a whole. The main strategy that will encourage sales after COVID-19 is reducing consumer pessimism by transitioning the brand's platform into a dialogue—one that does not focus on product or gain but that reminds people that we are all in this together.

A NOTE ON FASHION EDUCATION

This pandemic also marks a critical moment in the realm of fashion education. As the uncertainty of in-person education hangs in the air, it remains unforeseen how higher education will proceed. Enrollment will most likely decrease, and those who have the ability to attend will most likely remain close home; students will most likely fear straying too far from home in case another crisis occurs, meaning that the international student population will dwindle. We will see an emphasis placed on local businesses, activities, and goods. There will be a stronger focus on local production and cultivating a community through local events such as farmer's markets, small gallery openings, and an increasing number of artisanal studios. People will look to put down roots and utilize the services and resources around them. If people—especially young adults and students—find them unavailable, they will look to fill that gap in the market themselves. Fashion education, therefore, will need to shift into accommodating and bolstering young entrepreneurs, artisans, and craftspeople.

Italy is an exceptional example of a system that promotes quality, craftsmanship, and heritage, something of a novelty in the digital era. Italy's premiere fashion, art, and design schools feed this distinct system and keep it alive. Without this support of education, youth, and new innovation, the backbone of Italy's craft guilds would fracture, as evident in the disintegration of the American textile industry. It is important to note here that not only did America's man-ufacturing plants and labor market move overseas, but the entire garment industry as well; the garment industry includes textile manufacturers, tailors, and craftsmen that have an unparalleled knowledge of the construction behind, for instance, a true pair of American blue jeans.

Levi Strauss and Co. had its original factory in San Francisco before moving its production to Greensboro, North Carolina, once a haven for blue jean production with the likes of Lee, Wrangler, Blue Bell, and Cone producing their classic denim styles there as well.[4] To put it into numbers, according to *Business of Fashion*, in the 1960s, over 95 percent of apparel purchased in the United States was also made in the United States. With the creation of free trade laws beginning in the 1980s, the amount of clothing made overseas has drastically

---

4   Jeremy Markovich, "At Hudson's Hill, Denim is The Deepest Blue," *Our State*, August 5th, 2015.

increased; by 2015, roughly 97 percent of clothes sold in the US were imported from various countries around the globe.[5]

When we look to the future, we must see changes that decrease pollution and seek to end wasteful practices. The era of the mall and revering mass production is over, fashion shows will cease to exist on a massive scale, and we will turn to studios and showrooms that not only function as a platform for selling, but also serve as a base for collaborative projects such as workshops, seminars, and private tastings or parties. As a result, fashion schools must place an emphasis on product development and encourage classes in textiles, knitwear design, textile design, photography, and more so that students are prepared to start their own creative agencies and conduct every aspect in-house.

Unfortunately, we have not yet seen noticeable shifts in these areas. Instead, most innovation and change within the industry has been on a much smaller scale, and the rise of DTC (direct-to-consumer) brands seem wonderful with their creative and successful marketing techniques. However, just because a brand appears minimalistic and has a huge Millennial and Gen Z following does not mean that it is ethical.

There has been much discussion within the industry lately about reducing—if not completely doing away with—fashion shows. Designer Michael Kors has decided to leave fashion week altogether beginning with Spring/Summer 2021 at New York Fashion Week and is streamlining his collections to

---

5   Lauren Sherman, "Unravelling the Myth of 'Made in America,'" *Business of Fashion*, November 7th, 2016.

produce just two per year. Gucci's current creative director, Alessandro Michele, who is well-loved by the public for his inclusive principles, has also decided to streamline Gucci's presentations and call into question the sheer excess of fashion shows. It took a global pandemic for some of the biggest names in fashion to take a step back and look at the industry from a new perspective and think, "What are we doing here? What do we really need? Are we giving our consumers what they really need?" Many designers, founders, and creatives have been able to recognize that the frenzy for newness and consumption is not sustainable, and there is a very obvious need to return to the necessities, to the very birth of creation, and to the entire creative process. In turn, championing the creative process breeds cross collaboration and encourages production on a smaller scale.

These are four vital aspects to the fashion cycle, and they each must play a role in ethical business operations:

- materials
- manufacturing
- product
- people

MATERIALS
Truly, we must begin with a keen focus on materials that not only can endure, but also can be combined with technological innovations such as stress reducing fabrics, fabrics that can detect medical conditions, and fabrics that can keep you cool or warm you up. There are vast materials and innovations that have yet to be properly used and scaled due to lack of interest in investing in such endeavors.

Consumers are becoming even more tech-savvy and well-informed. Moving forward, they will demand more from the products and companies from which they choose to purchase. In an overcrowded marketplace over-saturated with advertisements and empty promises, it is key that a brand is able to differentiate itself. One of the most favorable ways to do so is through textile innovation and implementation. A stronger emphasis on literal life-changing fabrics and materials is exactly the truth and relevancy that consumers are searching for. Consumers are transitioning to purchases that are quite literally essential to their well-being, and if a fashion item does not fall in this category, then they will eventually not purchase it.

The beauty and wellness sectors are about to implode with a variety of brands seeking to persuade consumers in a new direction that looks satisfactory on paper and that is extremely marketable. For example, just last year, Gucci launched its own beauty line by utilizing a variety of models and celebrating inclusivity and diversity, two values that creative director Alessandro Michele aims to portray through all of the brand's channels.

MANUFACTURING
Following the importance of updated materials comes a selective manufacturing system. If companies and production become smaller and design shifts to in-house, then manufacturing can also remain local. If fashion brands reduce the number and size of collections they produce each year—specifically by not following the fashion show calendar—then the opportunity to downscale and focus on

creativity and consumer desires becomes more manageable. Consumer desires and needs are changing rapidly, and companies like Zara who operate a vertically integrated supply chain are one of few large brands that can easily adapt and shift production. Production on a smaller scale or in house allows brands to specifically tailor product to its consumers' needs and desires compared to a larger commercial company such as Zara. While Zara is vertically integrated, or oversees each stage of production from design to manufacturing, it is producing product for a broader market compared to a small brand that is able to interact with its consumers in a more personalized way via social media, in-person events, or through feedback surveys.

The current pandemic has provided a tremendous opportunity for both small and large brands to shift their production methods. If production becomes increasingly vertically integrated, more jobs and services will return in the United States to meet these needs, which will help local economies. Vertical integration is key in the apparel sector because it allows for companies to take total control over the creation of a good, from the design process all the way to the production and shipping to physical retail stores. Vertically integrating production will show companies that it is actually a more manageable method in terms of meeting consumer desires. Brands could also see increased consumer satisfaction as they would be employing members of local communities and contributing to local economies.

PRODUCT

As long as the products are high quality and meet consumer expectations, companies will see their actions paying off in terms of overall satisfaction and customer loyalty, a majorly difficult task to complete for both brands large and small. Mall retailers such as Gap and J. Crew have increasingly struggled in the past decade to deliver interesting product, and there has been movement away from previously popular 'all-American' brands to direct-to-consumer brands. These brands meet consumer needs through an efficient manner with uniform products that have interesting, inclusive, and interactive marketing strategies that rely heavily on digital platforms. A retailer such as J. Crew—which became popular in large part because its style of clothing imitates the upper class—is not an inclusive brand, meaning it does not resonate with a vast majority of consumers. J. Crew's brand message revolves around an aspiration to be upper-class compared to DTC brands like Warby Parker or luxury labels like Gucci that pioneer marketing campaigns with relatable people of all backgrounds and ages.

Brands with a compelling marketing effort not only focus on digital platforms, but their strategies are also differentiated across each individual platform to communicate with consumers in a new and exciting way each time. In this way, DTC brands spark conversation not so much focused on their product but more so on the inclusive community the consumers get to be a part of when they buy into the brand. This is a major selling aspect of consumers who are looking to connect with each other and the brands they favor in a digitally dominant world. Younger generations commonly look to their friends and family for recommendations on new products and use personal recommendations as their main source for choosing one product over another. Digital marketing initiates a chain of word-of-mouth interactions, which is the key to new sales.

PEOPLE

Interestingly but not surprisingly, the rise in digital strategies has also brought about a greater need for human interaction; a consumer wants to feel connected to a brand in a crowded online marketplace. The one true way to inspire a consumer purchase is to reach that consumer through a strong brand voice. DTC brands such as Warby Parker, Everlane, and Glossier have streamlined their product and marketing campaigns to repeatedly enforce their brand story and brand values.

Glossier runs campaigns featuring a diverse group of models wearing minimal makeup. Since their campaign features their own consumers wearing their product rather than incredibly intimidating and famous supermodels like Giselle, their campaigns relate directly to the consumer. In this way, a woman in her 20s or 30s can identify in a stronger capacity with an average woman wearing makeup than with a supermodel in fiery red lipstick in Vogue. Glossier's marketing fosters an emotional connection between the consumer and the brand. Furthermore, with their inclusive marketing strategies, the brand's core values of community, real life beauty, and conversation align and position the brand in the mind of the consumer.

From co-creating products directly with its consumer base to engaging in community talks and featuring its consumers in their marketing campaigns, Glossier is forming true human connections within the digital sphere. This kind of inclusion, diversity, and engagement drives a brand's success; a brand must realize that their consumers need to feel that their voice is heard and that they are a part of the brand in order to stand out in the flooded market. While Glossier is a beauty brand, the same is true for fashion brands struggling in the marketplace. In addition to having a relevant and exciting mix of product, an apparel brand must strive to form concrete bonds with its consumer base to weather the social, economic, and political uncertainties brought on by the pandemic.

CHAPTER 2

RENEWING THE AMERICAN DREAM

———

It has been almost a year since I lost my wonderful grandfather. In fact, as I write this, a year ago to the day we were tasting wine at a small fattoria in the outskirts of Florence. Even at age 93, he visited me in Florence with my mother and my aunt during the third semester of my second year abroad. Papa's family was from Catania, Sicily and he spoke the Catanese dialect of Italian. I happened to spend my fall semester abroad, studying Italian in Taormina, Sicily, close to where he was from. When my family visited, we went to Rome for a few days. Papa surprised us all by conversing with a taxi driver in a very thick dialect while I (blue eyes, blonde hair) chatted in proper Italian, and my mother (very dark hair, deeply tanned skin) interjected in exuberant American English. The Roman taxi driver could barely get a word in and was obviously confused as he strained to understand my grandfather who was gesturing wildly and speaking with the man as if they knew each other from childhood. Although Papa was the first child of the family to be born in the United States, he always exhibited the qualities of a true Italian: interested in authenticity, quality, and craftsmanship.

My grandfather was a tailor who grew up in East Boston, worked in the garment factories there, and raised his family all in the same city. He was extremely well-read and when he spoke, his strong voice and even cadence demanded attention. He could speak on a variety of subjects and had traveled to various parts of the world through his service on a submarine in World War II. Papa has a story like so many other Italian American immigrants—one characterized by hard work and a deep affection for his adopted country, yet strong ties to home. Papa continued to tailor even in retirement, working on family and friends' clothing. He kept his intricate Singer in our basement, and I would bring him coffee when he would come over to work. His stories always entertained and inspired me, but they would also serve to inspire my own dreams and passions.

Papa encouraged me to travel constantly, and once I chose fashion as my course of study, he decided I had to go to Hong Kong and learn about textiles. He emphasized the important work the Chinese mills were doing back in his day, and that he could only imagine the advancements and futuristic fabrics they were probably developing now. While I was unable to complete a semester in Hong Kong, I always remembered the ardent way in which he praised Chinese textile manufacturing.

As I consider his words now, I realize that Papa lived through the most prosperous and successful period in American textile manufacturing before factories shuttered nationwide and moved overseas. Papa bought bolts of fabric and made his own trousers and clothing, having a variety of patterns seemingly in his head. As a young child, the importance of these facts and the stories of American production seemed strange, especially since the Boston he spoke of and the one I knew seemed to be two different cities entirely.

The concept of American manufacturing and textile hubs is, of course, a very foreign subject for a young American who never knew Papa's America. I grew up shopping at Gap while fervently desiring the flashy fashions available at the Limited Too. I was accustomed to shopping malls and mass-produced clothing, knowing that if I saw another girl wearing a denim jacket with a butterfly patch, I could go to the mall and find the same jacket. I knew the concept of instant gratification well, and so did thousands of other Americans at a young age. Consumerism only grew worse as technology increasingly became integrated with everyday life and marketing and advertising moved away from a single creative campaign to digital media strategies that aim to bombard consumers in every aspect of everyday life.

The introduction of globalization to the integration of technology led to the offshoring of manufacturing, which completely changed the world and impacted the fashion industry in a profound way. Quite literally, America has lost the ability to make something for itself. The great ability of young Americans to maintain a fundamentally optimistic view of our country is, in my opinion, the very reason we are able to keep moving forward, albeit with little progress in the realm of fashion.

My grandfather not only had this optimism, persistence, and ambition, but also a great pride in his country that produced its clothing, its food, and educated its people. Now, the previous American factory workers are not working and are not even necessarily classified as unemployed.[6] These workers powered our nation to produce its own clothing and wares and have been left jobless. There are a diverse number of reasons for this, but we have reached a critical point in the industry and in the world as a whole that demands our attention and strategic solutions to the problem of outsourcing most of our manufacturing. Even the "American blue jean" is no longer an accurate descriptor since Japan has quickly risen to take America's place as the newest major hub of specialty denim production.

American manufacturing and artistry have almost completely disappeared, especially in the denim sector. Denim used to be produced in the United States. Even the cotton spun into denim was sourced in the southern United States. Levi's started in San Francisco and then moved its facilities to a denim mill hub in Greensboro, North Carolina, where a plethora of American denim brands also produced their products. Denim was originally the workingman's garment of choice, most often worn by and associated with farmers, mechanics, factory workers, and shopworkers in the 20s and 30s. World War II saw the rise in popularity of denim as millions of Americans, especially women, went to work in munitions factories to assist with the war.

---

6   Charles Murray, *Coming Apart: The State of White America 1960-2010* (New York, NY: Crown Publishing Group, 2012), 172-193.

Denim is a tough textile and can withstand constant wear and tear. In 1962, Levi's reported a peak in denim sales, a number that would soon soar going into the 70s. In Charles Reich's paean of 1960s counterculture, *The Greening of America*, he claims that jeans and 'informal clothing' was an expression of a new kind of consciousness, one that outrightly rejected the repressive American system and former rigid ways of life. Reich states, "They [jeans] are a deliberate rejection of the neon colors and plastic, artificial look of the affluent society. They are inexpensive to buy, inexpensive to maintain." [7] It is an interesting thought that jeans not only represent the individual, but also that they have come to represent America. This is precisely because jeans are more functional than other kinds of clothing.

Reich continues, "These clothes express freedom. Expensive clothes enforce social constraints; a grease spot on an expensive suit is a social error, so is a rip in a tailored ladies' coat, or a missing button. A man in an expensive suit must be careful of every move he makes, where he sits, what he leans against. A well-dressed woman is hardly able to walk or move. The new clothes give the wearer freedom to do anything he wants. He can work in them, read in them, roll down a hill in them, ride a bike in them, play touch football, dance, sit on the floor, go on a camping trip, sleep in them. Above all, they are comfortable. The freedom of new clothes expresses a second principle as well: a wholeness of self, as against the schizophrenia of Consciousness II. There is not one set of clothes for the office; another for social life, a third for play. The same clothes can be used for every imaginable

7   Charles A Reich, *The Greening of America* (New York: Bantam, 1971), 252.

activity, and so they say: it is the same person doing each of these things, not a set of different masks or dolls, but one many-sided, *whole* individual."[8]

After beginning my fashion education and traveling abroad, I now understand the concepts my grandfather spoke of on a new level. I can only imagine what he would have preached during this pandemic, and I can say for certain that he would have claimed that we needed a renewal of American-made local production and craftsmanship. I can practically hear him shouting at my dining room table about what a shame it is that our Levi's are not even made here. Papa was a proud tailor through and through and a loud Italian American with a very avant-garde approach. My grandfather's cries echo Li Edelkoort, a renowned Dutch trend forecaster's premonitions that the future of fashion—and now with the impacts of the pandemic—shall lead us back to the local. Edelkoort believes fewer students will be studying abroad, which in turn, will affect the nature of university. In her Special Edition Business of Fashion podcast, Edelkoort says, "That is going to be a big readjustment of the schools in terms of budget and general outlook. It might be good for the fashion industry because it will give back a local flavor and intention to the courses."[9]

Edelkoort claims the realities of the world today will shift us back into our national realms, and universities around

---

8   Charles A Reich, *The Greening of America* (New York: Bantam, 1971), 252–253.

9   Lidewij 'Li' Edelkoort, "Special Edition: Inside Fashion," March 27, 2020, in *The Business of Fashion Podcast*, produced by BoF, podcast, MP3 audio, 21:40-22:05.

the world will see an unmistakable decrease in their international student population. This will have profound effects on local areas as students seek education at universities in their hometowns along with the services, goods, and production that they can manage in such areas. There will be a new appreciation for the commodities that are pre-existing and ready for innovation. The return to the local will be unequivocal and exciting as young people begin to see the resources around them and use them in new ways. This is an indisputable shift that will bring American jobs. As a direct result, old American values such as industriousness will return.

CHAPTER 3

ALL IN AN INTERNSHIP

———

In the summer of 2018, I interned in women's merchandising at French Connection and also at Mish Fine Jewelry, a luxury, by-appointment-only jeweler. The following summer, I interned at AeroOp Co., now renamed SPARC group, which operates Aéropostale and Nautica. They placed me as the women's merchandising intern for Aéropostale and bounced me around between the lightweight knits, denim, outerwear, and swim/underwear teams—essentially every category of women's clothing that Aero designs and produces. The corporate Aero internship was exciting and fulfilling for multiple reasons; it encompassed my dream of working in merchandising, of being in New York City, of learning how each team (from merchandising to design to product development) interacted, and what a corporate fashion structure really looked like.

Both Aero and Nautica interns were placed in the same intern 'class.' We participated in a variety of events together such as Excel courses, design meetings, interview and job search preparation, scavenger hunts, and bring your lunch and learn dates. I was very fortunate to be one of two Marist students in this cohort amongst a mixture of brilliant and diverse FIT, Cornell, and Yale students. As a group of thirteen, we were divided into the departments of merchandising, design, planning & allocation, and marketing based on our course of study. Despite all of our different backgrounds and focuses, we all shared the same naive passion that seems to possess young creatives. This quality is almost palpable in a group of fashion-forward interns, and even more so in the Gen Z cohort: we all have uninhibited ambition.

I greatly admired my fellow interns, especially the talented designers who boasted impressive résumés at some of the top salons in the city, which I understood was not only due to FIT's location, but to their persistence to change the design cycle. While all of the design interns championed the same sustainability tactics as my friend Isabel, they also fiercely debated the notion of sustainability and how it should be defined. One of the design interns argued that it is just another favorite buzz word in the industry at the moment. Another intern, wearing a gorgeous Milly dress, defended the structures taken up by popular brands such as Everlane and Reformation, although it was curious that she left out Stella McCartney and Patagonia. I should point out that these conversations would begin casually and would quickly bring everyone to the table, inviting a variety of opinions to mesh together. It was not necessarily pretty to look at, but it was intriguing, nonetheless.

These conversations would come to a halt as soon as our collective internship supervisors descended upon the room. What I liked about our unfiltered conversations was the raw honesty with which we interns, from a variety of disciplines and backgrounds, spoke. It was also amusing to hear the personal opinions about Aero and Nautica's operations in front of the CEO's daughter, who happened to be a brilliant planning intern with us that summer. It seemed that everyone had a pure passion to make the industry better; instituting some aspect of change seemed to outweigh any consequences of speaking openly. For the first time since I began college, I was reminded of my high school Advanced Placement courses, which year after year consisted of the same ambitious and intelligent students arguing every point and presenting new ideas and facts to mull over. Our little intern class was actually a very liberating space in which we could discuss the realities of the fashion landscape we faced, not only as future industry professionals, but also as consumers.

One day, we were assembled to discuss new Aero marketing ideas for their sustainable denim collection that would be released the next year. A variety of important figures such as the head of design, the head of concept and color, and the creative director were in attendance as well. I thought that no one would end up volunteering their opinions in this slightly intimidating meeting, but I was wrong. The discussion slowly picked up its pace as we went through slides displaying new marketing materials and slogans that would promote the new denim material and voted on our favorites. We were all aware of our surroundings, yet we voted for our favorites even if we were the only ones, feeling the prickly sense of fear when we were asked to explain our choice. Everyone who came up with the ideas we were judging were crowded in the back of the conference room, observing us and whispering to each other about which intern opinions they disregarded and which actually had value to them.

Soon the topics escalated from slogan approvals to the concept of sustainability itself and whether or not the company was heading in the right direction. They asked us if sustainability was relevant with its consumer base, which sparked a heated debate amongst us. I remember one particular intern taking a strong stance for environmentally friendly textiles and the need to do more. She praised brands that had instituted ethical sourcing, radical transparency, and quality product. She was persistent that this route was the future of fashion and that Aero needed to take more initiative to align themselves with brands like these and to implement stricter production standards. However, this intern failed to recognize something that I read on the faces of the directors behind us: Aero could not simply terminate their manufacturing contracts with factories in Cambodia and Vietnam for ethically certified ones in China or elsewhere. Drastic changes in sourcing and production would be accompanied by a massive upcharge and an increase in prices that the Aero consumer would not only be unwilling to pay but also unable to understand.

The customer looking to buy their growing child's back to school jeans for $20 cannot rationalize a price shift to $50, especially if there are other children in the family. Before I knew it, I had raised my hand. I called for the education of the consumer before drastic changes could be implemented, despite my strong beliefs in quality over quantity. I argued that by morphing into an Everlane or Reformation who target a vastly different consumer base, Aero would drive its consumer away to off-price retailers such as T.J.Maxx or Ross. Aero operates on a discount model that other mall retailers such as American Eagle, Abercrombie, Hollister, and Garage use. If you took away mall retailers, you would be left with two kinds of retailers: luxury conglomerates and off-price retail giants. These two kinds of retailers are representative of two kinds of consumer segments in America: the upper class is the luxury brands, and the lower class is the off-price retailers.

As I sat in that board room considering the planet's cry for help, intense consumer greed, and the vast measures that need to be taken to continue to create in our beautiful industry, I could not help but wonder if the answers were already out there. America is the land of the free, the home of the brave, and a country that fosters entrepreneurship and innovation, yet where is the innovation in fashion? Where is the collective interest to renew a massive industry that has become so backward?

Throughout my four years of college, I have noticed a startling difference between the fashion education teaching models in the United States and Europe. I studied for two years in Italy and for two years in the Hudson Valley. I also visited friends as they studied at a fashion design and merchandising university in Paris and admired their projects and work.

What is the difference between these American and European models? Well, simply put, one encourages innovation and the other one does not. One pushes you to find answers outside of fashion and apply them to your project, and the other one throws knowledge at you and hopes you absorb it. In the European model, textile science is a fascinating and difficult but an immersive experience, but in the American model it is terrifying and something to quickly put behind you. This, I fear, is where we begin to go in the wrong direction, one where there is little understanding and hope for the future of fashion.

Back at Aero, we were a cohort of thirteen passionate and intelligent students, and we all agreed upon the massive problem our industry currently faces: excess. This problem not only pertains to those within the fashion industry—it applies to the entire world. We are all consumers, we are all contributors to the problem, and we can only solve this if we work together. There will always be a desire for something new that fuels demand and makes this industry so mighty and powerful. However, there has to be a new, more efficient way to accumulate not only new belongings, but those that are able to withstand years' worth of wearing and washing. This is not a groundbreaking idea either; companies such as L.L. Bean and Patagonia were founded to create well-made gear that can withstand years of use. We have few answers to the crisis the fashion industry faces today, but we will not overcome it with marketing efforts alone; there must be call for a collective shift in our consumer mindset that will enable the industry to transform, renew, and grow.

We cannot blame consumers for their ignorance about textiles and the massive lies the industry leads them to believe. Our fashion students, journalists, and industry leaders are certainly at fault. We must educate others and push for higher standards that empower and serve us. If our journalists cannot report thoroughly on textiles and if our fashion students cannot tell a knit from a woven, how will a consumer ever understand the markup on premium textiles? How can a consumer understand the conscious choice of purchasing $20 denim versus $200 premium selvedge denim? These answers are not readily available for consumers. These answers are not reported—let alone understood—by fashion professionals.

The new business model concepts that fashion must consider begin at its core with textiles. Until recently, textiles had always been the center of the industry. Before, in the 1950s or even 1960s, textiles were valued much more than they are today. These carefully sourced and spun fibers allowed our clothing to last longer. There are fortunately a few meccas left such at Italy, which brave the fight to save artisanal goods and quality spun yarns.

Why has this happened? Well, to begin with, through the Great Depression there was little to no consumer spending power for ready-to-wear clothing. Instead, consumers would buy fabric and make their own clothing. They created these garments with the intention of making them last a very long time and withstand working, washing, scrubbing, and drying. Consumers therefore needed to have a profound knowledge of textiles, including which ones had key properties of durability, softness, and water resistance. When the mass production of clothing increased after World War II, and lowered prices, the demand for artisanal or homemade, one-of-a-kind goods significantly dropped.

Fast forward to the offshoring of American textile and clothing manufacturing combined with a greater demand for newness and low-price points, and the artisanal goods market has all but disappeared. The one-of-a-kind products and garments available are increasingly expensive since they are produced on a small scale through small businesses. This justification is difficult for consumers who have become accustomed to purchasing the low-cost recreation of a hot ticket runway item at a mass retailer. It becomes unfathomable for a consumer to pay over $200 for trousers when they could buy similar ones that cost $40. People must realize that those gorgeous $200 trousers can be worn over and over again and can live in a closet for 10-15 years. In contrast, the $40 trousers are not made of carefully sourced fabric and will only withstand up to a year's worth of wash and wear before being tossed into a landfill. To completely shift this consumer mindset, we must also evolve fashion's primary business model.

The primary step in forming another business model first revolves around improving the industry's understanding of and value placed upon textiles and textile production. Next, we must empower our fashion journalists and leading professionals to the importance of buying quality and slow goods and what repercussions these purchases have on our environment and our future. Education is a vital part of initiating a new business model because it is the key to creating a collaborative mindset—one focused on slow fashion, essential goods, and quality textiles. Once this mindset shifts, we can begin to overhaul the structure of sourcing, manufacturing, and design.

Once we are able to shift consumers' mindsets and understanding, we can build the foundation of the new business structure—one defined by collaboration rather than individualism. There are already some innovative business models within the industry such as the rental model and the consignment model that have a very fluid business structure that promotes sharing, inclusivity, and collaboration. In these models, fashion is like one large closet that belongs to everyone. While these are wonderful models, they need to be able to scale in the future to see widespread growth and adoption of these practices. In the front of production, however, we will need to create a business model that operates upon shared designs, perhaps with outposts throughout the world which work in tandem with sourcing and manufacturing to produce specialty products.

Li Edelkoort is strongly in favor of an open source design center which fosters creativity and reduces the need for design and product developers to fly around the world in search of a manufacturer that can produce a cheaper replication of a luxury item.[10] While this is the exact mindset we want to change, it will not happen right away. Instead, we have to come up with solutions that can tamper down the excess waste produced within the existing industry.

First, we need to begin incubation programs for students that enable talented designers, chemists, and merchandisers to come together and problem solve. Veja, a footwear and accessories brand started by French duo François-Ghislain Morillion and Sébastien Kopp, is on a mission to revamp the sneaker scene with their environmentally friendly kicks. The brand creates their sneakers by sourcing each of their components individually from small cotton farms in Brazil and using new materials that resemble leather. The attention to

---

10   Lidewij 'Li' Edelkoort, "Special Edition: Inside Fashion," March 27, 2020, in *The Business of Fashion Podcast*, produced by BoF, podcast, MP3 audio, 34:00-34:40.

detail in developing their sneakers goes far beyond the chic style you see on their store shelves; Veja is transforming the way a consumer shops for a sneaker. Veja's website walks one through the ethos of the company and then displays how their raw materials are sourced, crafted, and materialized into a shoe. This kind of radical transparency is exactly what appeals to the new consumer mindset post-COVID-19 and amidst the turbulent social and political backdrops across the globe today. In 2019, Veja launched their first running shoe, which took four years of research and development to bring to fruition. Despite knowing of Veja and owning a pair myself, there was a lack of coverage on the company's magnificent strides in the footwear arena. The only thorough article I found about their new running line made out of rice waste, banana oil, sugar cane, and recycled plastic bottles comes from the online *Fashion Journal* based in Australia. The short article written by Mariah Papadopoulos lists the natural materials used to create the shoe and applauds Veja for their plastic reduction initiatives. Unfortunately, this is slight press for a shoe and a company that is actively creating healthier sneakers for our environment.[11] In an article by Elizabeth Segran for Fast Company, she relays how Kopp said "We had to learn about each component that was used to make a sneaker… There are only three: leather, rubber, and canvas, which is made from cotton. And we decided we would find the most sustainable version of each of these raw materials."[12]

---

11 Mariah Papadopoulos, "Veja's first line of running shoes is made from rice waste, sugar cane and banana oil," *Fashion Journal,* September 24, 2019.

12 Elizabeth Segran, "Veja Wants to Make the Most Sustainable Sneaker in the World," *Fast Company,* March 6th, 2018.

Dover Street Market, which fosters new designers across the globe and aids the development of new, small batch collections that are available worldwide at their markets for a limited amount of time. This is a new method which attracts consumers back to the brick and mortar, gives aspiring designers opportunity, and garners attention with an alternate model that rejects the grandiose style of a typical fashion show and its rigid calendar.

Edelkoort has taught in fashion programs and is specifically known for teaching one that takes place over the summers in Marseilles and focuses on the creation of new business models. She notes that fashion is curiously trapped in the 20th century; we are in the 21st century without any new innovation or model to show for it. The fashion cycle has become incredibly outdated, and now we must focus on a return to the old, tested, and true.

The notion of slow fashion—the all-encompassing idea of the curated and the handmade with a human story—should be at the very core of a new business model. The return of fashion to the artisan and the craft will be marked by an increase in personalization and a narrative of humanity and emotion; consumers will increasingly want to see and feel the emotion and the personal story of the person who created their new denim, their ceramic bowl, and their linen trousers. This business model will be considerably smaller and will be tailored to a personal and intimate telling of a designer's story and passions. There is room for the existing models to also gain from personalization and the human narrative, possibly through carefully curated 'closet picks' or video chat styling.

After this pandemic, the human connection will be more important than ever before, as will beauty and wellness. We'll see more collections, brands, and advertisements popping up in this sector of the industry, but although consumers will be more health-conscious, brands will not necessarily see immediate success. A brand moving forward will only survive the tumultuous times through increased awareness surrounding its product and consumer segment. A brand must now be able to tap into human emotion not only to help them deliver valuable, high-quality product, but also to offer key interactions with the brand outside the realm of purchasing. These interactions could be targeted Instagram posts, Live sessions, Zoom seminars, or intimate, by-appointment-only in-store events focused on a curated topic. Furthermore, brands and business models must incorporate the idea of returning to living a good, slow life in order to attract tech-savvy and quality-concerned consumers.

Along this line of thinking, the possibilities for experiential showrooms to blossom is immense. Brands could look to open small store fronts that actually serve as a way to interact with a brand and its ambassadors or creative director. This experiential brick and mortar would, in turn, increase online traffic and lead to sales. The key to an experiential showroom would be to create and fulfill the experience that the name suggests, not to push product.

CHAPTER 4

THE RENTAL MODEL

———

The rental model has emerged as one of the new business structures that fashion so desperately needs. This model has actually existed for longer than most consumers are aware of, as it originated as the brainchild of Harvard Business School Entrepreneurs Jennifer Hyman and Jenny Fleiss in 2008. The two students originally created the Rent the Runway online platform and business model as a way to cater to women looking for gowns and cocktail dresses that they only needed for a singular occasion. The rental model even allows women to rent a pair of the same gown in different sizes, to ensure that they find the right fit for their event. While their singular dress rental is a component of their business, their core business comes from their monthly Unlimited subscription service, which gives consumers access to a vast array of product for only $159 a month.[13]

The idea behind the rental model is ingenious to say the least. Rent the Runway is undoubtedly the most successful example

---

13   Chavie Lieber, "The Fashion Rental Market Tested and Explained: Who Has the Best Service?" *Business of Fashion,* February 5th, 2020.

of this business model and operates directly out of New York City. At first, consumers only slowly welcomed this model, although they applauded it for its originality and eco-friendly tactics that worked against the excess of production by utilizing left-over inventory. This model had such a slow start because it was targeting Millennials, Gen X-ers, and Boomers. Out of these three generational cohorts, Millennials are the most likely to adopt this clothing practice because, generally speaking, they are open to change, value teamwork, and are extremely tech savvy. For a diverse group of consumers who are open to change but want things immediately (instant gratification), a rotating weekly wardrobe of new garments is the perfect answer to their demands.

While Millennials take risks and are very responsive to word of mouth communication, the older two cohorts, however, need more persuasion to adopt something so new. If a Millennial hears a friend or reads a blog post praising Rent the Runway, they would be more likely to test the company's services than a Gen X-er or Baby Boomer would be.

Despite the ethical and environmental solutions the rental model provides, there is a serious question of the high costs of upkeep for rental goods, and the supply chain must also be efficient for consumers, as they would cancel their subscriptions if it becomes a hassle to receive and exchange their items. In order to make the processes more convenient, Rent the Runway has recently collaborated with other retailers such as West Elm to act as drop boxes for their subscriptions. Another issue surrounding the rental model is the high costs for consumers; unlimited subscriptions cost upwards of $160 per month and student plans cost around $89 per month, although this plan does not include unlimited swapping and only includes a small selection of items.

Myriad brands utilize the rental platform company, CaaStle, to run their own shops, in an attempt to maintain control over their brand image and narrative rather than joining Rent the Runway. National retailers that use CaaStle range from Vince and Rebecca Taylor to American Eagle Outfitters, Anne Taylor, among others. The reoccurring issue with a brand's own rental service stems from poor management of a customer's wish list that results from a lack of inventory. For example, on Rebecca Taylor's rental platform, subscribers put together a rack of 24 ranked items they wish to receive. Out of the 24 items, customers are sent 4 pieces from their selection, but they have no control over what pieces they will actually end up with; if their top-ranked products are unavailable, customers will receive various items ranked low on their wish list that they did not necessarily want. In contrast, on Rent the Runway, you are guaranteed the 4 items you select. The most disappointing part about receiving random 4 items is that they are most often just that: a random selection instead of the specially curated outfit pieces that the consumer had chosen to wear for the month. The lack of variety in items that can be paired together can cause problems for consumers who do not necessarily have other items in their closet to supplement their random rental items.

If the rental model is supposed to be the solution to a fully stocked wardrobe, then why are brands unable to deliver the items the consumer specifically chose to wear together? We can instead view the subscription service as a way for consumers to inject fashion pieces into their wardrobe. Many rental platforms have found that consumers still invest in essential goods and use their subscriptions to test out trendier, more expensive items.

In this sense, multi-brand retailers such as Nuuly—the rental platform by URBN featuring brands such as Urban Outfitters, Free People, and Anthropologie—have an advantage over a singular brand like Rebecca Taylor Or Vince. Nuuly offers over 100 third-party brands in addition to their mainstay brands. Some of their exciting third-party labels include LoveShackFancy and Levi's, and they also curate a special offering of vintage clothing—everything from Levi's to Yves Saint Laurent. As a result, struggling retailers are seeking options in the rental realm; Bloomingdale's has been the first department store to show interest in launching its own rental service.

Dry cleaning is one of the costliest aspects to running a subscription rental service. It takes a considerable chunk of investment to set up specialty dry cleaning facilities around the country that correctly wash the garments, dry them, and ship them out again. Additionally, some garments need specialty cleaning, mending, or multiple washes because an odor has lingered. Despite these costs, the rental service has to remain dedicated to its ethical mission and use more expensive, eco-friendly washing and drying techniques since standard dry cleaning does not actually clean the garment thoroughly enough.

In addition to high operational costs, many subscription services find difficulty in retaining customers; as the novelty eventually wears off, consumers unsubscribe completely or test out a new platform. Retention is important in this case, as profit only results from customer loyalty and the maintaining subscriptions. This disregard for brand loyalty is a character trait of the young consumer, therefore URBN designed Nuuly with this knowledge in mind. Dave Hayne, Chief Digital Officer at Urban Outfitters and president of Nuuly, says of the Nuuly structure, "We want to make this offering as easy as Netflix is—pause and cancel and come back in." This attitude and approach to the rental model is the most advisable one considering the consumer mindset and the fact that a subscription service is a high-investment, long term evolution that will require expansion into other product categories that will continue to appeal to consumers and encourage them to keep renewing their subscriptions.

Despite these negative aspects, the positives to the rental model are immense and help prove that the rental model is a worthwhile investment. Dry cleaning costs, customer service, and pricing aside, the rental subscription is one of the most ethical choices a consumer can make to refill their closet while consciously reducing consumption. Rent the Runway used to buy excess merchandise from major brands each season, but now they have brands approaching them to put their new merchandise on the site. This change is a direct result of lacking wholesale account sales. Retailers such as Macy's, J.C. Penney, and other regional department stores are suffering major profit losses due to reduced foot traffic in-store and outdated business models, therefore weakening wholesale brands that typically sell through large retailers. While the wholesale model has all but been destroyed by the change in buying habits due to COVID-19, the model was heavily distressed before the pandemic erupted across the globe. Consumer buying habits have changed due to a myriad of reasons, and once popular retailers are struggling to keep up with rapidly changing consumer taste.

Contrary to what you may think, the rental model does not decrease consumer sales, but actually encourages more of them; consumers buy essential goods to match the clothing they rent and sometimes even purchase the merchandise after they rent it. Since many subscribers rent fashion pieces rather than essential pieces, they are essentially using a subscription service to have access to high-quality, trendy fashion pieces that they would not normally purchase. They still must purchase everyday items like sweatshirts, intimates, denim, and other basic tees and tanks.

The rental model does a wonderful job of offering newness and of collecting unused merchandise from various brands across the industry. It also encourages consumers to stock their wardrobe with only the necessary pieces to wear on a day off and keeps them from filling their closets with frivolous pieces from Zara that replicate and capitalize upon luxury designers' gorgeous, creative work. The rental model also introduces consumers to new designers and luxury items; they now have a direct way of accessing an $800 shift dress that they could never afford as an outright purchase. By introducing consumers to designer clothing, there is a subtle but detectable shift in the consumer mindset; the consumer understands that their rented denim fits their thighs better not just simply because of the label, but because the fabric is noticeably better.

Before, this consumer might have said, "What's the difference between my Zara jeans and your Rag and Bone jeans? There isn't a difference!" Now, however, this consumer visibly sees and feels the difference, and no longer can say that a pair of jeans is just a pair of jeans. Their new knowledge of fabric properties and labels can lead to new shopping methods for the consumer. No, this consumer still cannot afford $300 jeans, but she can afford to go to her local vintage shop and scour the racks for an old pair of Rag and Bone ones that have been marked down. I believe the rental model can actually fuel the vintage model, which is another revolutionary step toward breaking the fashion cycle, but—like with the rental model—only if more consumers are willing to adopt it.

The rental model could borrow strategies from the vintage model and offer inventory sales to sell their old rented product or set up a curated, experiential showroom that actually has stylists who put together old pieces and work with clients. As we shift to personalization and deeper human interaction, the rental and vintage models can feed off of this return to slow fashion and emotion by fostering communities in which consumers get together and share clothes, advice, or coffee. By creating a unique experience that ties women and their closets together, both of these models have the ability to widen their consumer base.

In order to sustain itself, the rental model also must adjust for their Gen Z consumers. A $125-$150 a month payment is neither feasible nor rational when students are paying for transportation to their internships, dues for club soccer, or travelling to career networking events in Washington DC. Of course, some rental options give consumers the ability to rent particular items of clothing for a certain amount of time, but to truly target Gen Z and the generational cohort below them and maintain their business, this is simply not the right tactic. Instead, there must be a student offer through which the young consumer can discover and learn about new brands, textiles, and ethical production.

The entire fashion industry must adapt to the student since this particular consumer is the all-encompassing revolutionary in the economy as a whole. The young, educated mind has the power to disrupt and institute change, especially when change is so desperately needed. It is shocking, indeed, that the very creators of these sites do not recognize or even exclude Gen Z-ers for sake of profit.

Ignoring Gen Z-ers is a massive miscalculation; a student package would create a loyal following, especially with Gen Z members who are attracted to authentic brand voices, eco-friendly and ethical missions, and inclusivity. What better way to foster inclusivity and attract loyal subscribers than by offering them a tailored package that allows them access to new clothing while also caring for their planet? Instead, I see many students—fashion and other disciplines alike—raiding vintage stores, secondhand clothing websites, and used luxury goods shops. Since the rental model has rejected a vital consumer segment, another fashion business model has been given the opportunity to flourish: the consignment model.

CHAPTER 5

THE CONSIGNMENT MODEL

—

Inside, the excitement is tangible. The smell is old. What is it? Mothballs? Grandma's coat? Either way, the racks and displays ignite tiny lights in my eyes as I wander through the vintage store, looking for nothing in particular. This is one of my favorite places. I walk around quickly, my eyes darting over everything, deciding where to begin. My eyes finally settle on a rack of bright blue jeans hanging by their belt loops. My fingers graze each pair, swiftly passing through the beloved brands. My hand closes around a dark wash pair designed by Italian designer, Adriano Goldschmeid, the "Godfather of Denim," and I smile. I know they will be coming home with me this afternoon.

I am from a blue-collar city on the outskirts of Boston—a city ripe with achievements in medicine, technology, and higher education. The city I live in is very diverse yet segregated into very different parts. The public high school I attended and the classes I took are very much the same as the layout of the city itself. I note this because it is important to understand the context in which I am speaking: the context of vintage clothes. As a child, I knew of second-hand clothes and shared the same arrogant attitude toward them that Gen X and Boomers maintain.

When I was in high school, however, I learned more about second-hand clothes from a very artsy and brilliant classmate with whom I shared a variety of classes. In high school, it is a novelty when someone wears something radically different than expected (although I suspect this has changed a lot in the years since I have graduated). Every day, this classmate wore interesting clothes and even I—a ridiculously meticulous shopper—could not identify their origins. I was fascinated but irritated to the point where I would ask where she found her jacket or what her shoes were called.

Her answers led me on a new path that I have yet to leave behind, and I become increasingly intrigued by another facet of the fashion world. She was, of course, shopping at a variety of vintage and second-hand shops, and even some yard sales. It would take me two more years to finally enter a consignment shop in a very wealthy town nearby which, to my delight, had a rack of designer denim all in my size! Thus began my trips to find Mother, Rag & Bone, and One-Teaspoon jeans for $30 a pair until my mother realized where my work money was going and demanded that something be done.

To pacify my mother, I decided to begin selling my old clothes and, in turn, use the credit to buy other items at the shop. I created my own little fashion cycle. Another reason

I was so compelled to return to the little shop was the sheer thrill of finding something unexpected and investigating a new label or shape of clothing. I knew that if I didn't realize the items my classmate was wearing, there was surely a whole slew of garments and shoe styles that I had yet to hear of. The consignment shop was not only a place to purchase cool jeans for a fraction of the price, but it was also a portal into the past—into '90s silhouettes, vintage Chanel, and old Tiffany styles. I was simultaneously gaining access to current styles while increasing my knowledge of the past and beginning to understand how vintage styles related to the new product on runways and in mass retailers.

Another of my favorite aspects of this little haven was their window displays, which continued to captivate me. In an adorable New England town, this unassuming little brick shop with white paneling had the most creative and appealing windows I had ever seen. Oftentimes, I would go in and try on what I saw on the window mannequins. If one of the pieces did not fit, I would look for something similar somewhere else. Since shop associates rotated schedules, I did not meet the visual merchandiser for a while. I must have made an impression though, because the next time I was trying on window pieces, she seemed to know exactly who I was.

My shopping excursions that followed our meeting always began with a phone call from her telling me she had the coolest midi denim skirt (a few years before they were really popular), a billowy white linen shirt, or Dior slingbacks in my size (I still regret not getting those sweet Dior heels). She was a true stylist, through and through. Of course, she had another job, but she did this one so well not only because she enjoyed it and had an eye for it, but because she provided a personalized shopping experience for customers. Just as the store associates at Bergdorf's will call their wealthy clients and notify them of The Row's new collection or a suit that would be perfect for them, this associate used her rapidly changing influx of inventory to sell pieces and get more pieces in return. She knew what her customers likedand just what we might be in search of.

This type of shopping experience is the exact kind of personalization that will make a comeback post COVID-19. This sales tactic represents the return to a human connection and is a representation of the joy, creativity, and beauty of fashion that has been missing in the retail world for quite some time. Many consumers are not in search of something particular, and in a market oversaturated with goods, brand names, and advertisements, it is nearly impossible to see through the noise and decipher what we actually want. By presenting the consumer with something they might be searching for, they not only excite the consumer but actually encourage interaction and—if the stylist knows their customer—earn a successful sale.

It is difficult to know which brands are honest, which products are high quality, and where you should feel good about shopping. A stylist takes care of these concerns for you, and everyone would probably want one if they could afford them. There will always be stylists for a wealthy clientele that operate solely in the luxury realm, but what if there was someone who managed the rest of the world's closet? What if the vintage community became the next hub of stylists and trend-setting individuals?

A consignment or vintage shop is a wonderful business model that truly has the opportunity to not only change the way consumers interact with garments but also influence buying habits. The next decade in fashion will prove critical to innovate with new and current business models in order to change consumer buying patterns.

Unfortunately, I can see one particular catch in regards to this business model that I believe is drastically affecting its ability to grow and occupy a legitimate position in consumers' minds: there are a very large number of consumers who are not interested in purchasing second hand clothing. This specific group of consumers is usually within older generational cohorts and view purchasing of second-hand clothing to be sort of mockery of their accomplishments. This cohort views their ability to purchase clothing as a symbol of wealth. In the time period in which Gen X was raised, used clothing or 'hand me downs' were often associated with the lower classes. Now, however, Millennials and Gen Z-ers have reversed that ideology and recognize that used clothing can be trendy, cool, and an ethical, affordable way to refresh their wardrobes. Used clothing is a sustainable method of consumption because it does not put new material into the market, but rather creates a circular cycle that moves clothing around some of the largest metropolitan areas of the world.

Despite the abundance of vintage shops in fashion forward cities such as New York, London, and Berlin, there are many gems to be found in small shops in suburban areas or in massive Salvation Army superstores. The hunt for a particular vintage garment requires the time and energy to search through racks as well as an extensive knowledge of brands, silhouettes, and styles to identify rare pieces. I feel that many people shy away from this hunt because of the sheer amount of work it entails; it is certainly not an instant gratification process in which you see an item, like it, and purchase it on the spot. Another difficult aspect of buying vintage is never knowing what you may find; you cannot necessarily go in search of one particular piece. Instead, you must begin your search with a clear mind and an excitement for what you may find. Often times, the piece finds you.

The concept of Nasty Gal, a major online retailer, actually began this way; Nasty Gal started as a vintage online eBay shop founded by Sophia Amoruso, who had an innate knack for style and an ability to find and recognize one-of-a-kind pieces. Her business quickly grew, and rather than continuing in the vintage sector, the brand took off as an online retailer that borrowed styles from high-quality goods and joined the ranks of mass production fashion for young women. The decline of a niche vintage shop with a passionate founder into yet another fast fashion retailer among the ranks of Boohoo and Misguided is a tragedy in and of itself for the major loss to the vintage market. The appeal of vintage currently stands as a trendy option for stylish young adults and teenagers interested in quality goods, past silhouettes, and paying less than the original retail price. In order to see the appeal and proper growth of the vintage mindset, a few adjustments must first be made to the model.

CHAPTER 6

FASHION SHOULD
NEVER GO TO WASTE

What do consumers do with beautiful designer pieces sitting in their closets, unworn? Sophie Hersan and five co-founders created a solution for this problem with Vestiaire Collective, a luxury vintage resale company.[14] The founders came up with the idea for Vestiaire Collective from watching the gorgeous designer garments of their friends swaying, forsaken, in their closets. In 2009, the six co-founders created a platform that would allow consumers to buy and sell luxury goods, and now the company has gone global with a team of 400+ employees.

Hersan says of their ambitious start, "Our early vision was focused on embedding circularity at the heart of the fashion industry and consumer mindset by building a community for fashion activists around the world, creating a sustainable

---

14 Ann Binlot, "Vestiaire Collective Celebrates a Decade in Luxury Resale," *Forbes,* December 31st, 2019.

solution for selling pieces they [the consumers] no longer needed." The beginning of Vestiaire Collective was something of a novelty in a marketplace that had no solution for used luxury goods. Hersan notes, "It really disrupted the fashion ecosystem by driving changes in the way we consume fashion: to consume less, better and smarter."

According to Hersan, the idea of consuming "less, better, and smarter" is the exact mindset for which the entire fashion industry must strive towards. The planet cannot sustain the industry's turnover, over-consumption, and consumers' desperation for renewing their wardrobes every season. The vintage resale market provides ample opportunities for consumers to explore fashion and satisfy their desire for newness in their wardrobes; according to Hersan, "resale gives fashion lovers the opportunity to extend the lifespan of their own items while also allowing them to explore other people's unique, pre-loved items. It is an exciting, dynamic market that offers a much more sustainable approach to fashion."

The major issue with many of the fast fashion retailers is that their garments are so poorly constructed that they barely last a season in a consumer's wardrobe, never mind being able to last thirty years down the road. If all garments were constructed equally and made with attentiveness to quality and textiles, then the state of the fashion industry would be much different. Unfortunately, the industry accelerated at an unhealthy pace and has deliberately become flooded with millions of cheap articles of clothing and retailers chase money at the expense of consumers and of our planet.

Hersan sees this detrimental flaw within the industry and describes how Vestiaire has transformed in the new marketplace while remaining true to their founding virtues. She says that sustainability has always been "at the heart of Vestiaire Collective- we recently hired Chief Sustainability and Inclusivity Officer Dounia Wone who is going to guide the company moving toward a path of more sustainable development." Hersan and the other founders of Vestiaire Collective aren't necessarily re-inventing the wheel, but rather finding an opportunity to cultivate consumers' passions for exquisite pieces while encouraging the circular fashion system at the same time.

Circular fashion eliminates waste and pollution in order to boost the lifecycle of products and materials through a variety of processes so that a garment may circulate amongst its users for as long as possible. Retail giants such as Zara, Walmart, Gap, and others are not interested in extending a garment's lifecycle for as long as possible, as they fear it would in turn result in less consumption, fewer people in stores, and less overall profit. Vintage, on the other hand, especially on the luxury end, thrives off of this extensive lifecycle; a Vestiaire consumer is ecstatic to find a matching Versace set from the '80s or a Margiela skirt from the early 2000s. Not only are they excited to find an iconic piece from a legendary designer, but they are also elated to have a quality garment that has already witnessed several lifetimes and has several more to go.

I asked Hersan about the major shifts we are seeing in consumer behavior and the resulting movements such as slow food and slow fashion, specifically whether or not she thought these movements propel interest within the resale market. She confirmed "Yes, absolutely. The resale market has boomed in response to a shift in the consumer mindset about the impact their wardrobe has on the environment and the way they buy fashion. There is a clear departure from 'ownership' [which] answers the addiction to newness as more prioritized usage over possession." This departure is crucial, especially post COVID-19, since various challenges and opportunities have erupted for all fashion brands.

Hersan notes, "Since the outbreaks, we did have some initial setbacks because many of our key markets have been impacted by the outbreak, but as a C2C [consumer to consumer] platform, we make adjustments to the way we operate quite quickly, and as a result, we were able to bounce back and actually see growths in both orders and deposits compared to last summer." Hersan describes the growth Vestiaire has seen through the company's recently launched *Smart Side of Fashion* report which details various trends amongst Vestiaire's community of 10 million.[15] She says, "one of our findings was that vintage as a category has recorded a tremendous growth in sales. For example, vintage Prada recorded a 40 percent increase in sales, while Margiela had a 65 percent increase and Miu Miu saw a 21 percent increase." These are major increases, especially when you consider the fact that the vintage market was previously only accessible through brick and mortar stores. Vestiaire Collective was able to appeal to an entirely new consumer segment by creating a digital platform for consumers to shop.

---

15 "The Smart Side of Fashion," Vestiaire Collective, accessed June 2020.

The post-Coronavirus market presents its own set of challenges and opportunities, but Hersan acknowledges the company performed well throughout the global pandemic, even with the Paris head office and most of the regional offices functioning remotely. Hersan believes the world will gain a different viewpoint in the post COVID-19 era; "they [the consumers] might reconsider their priorities and the way they consume, [and] the McKinsey COVID-19 response in Apparel and Fashion study stated that 20 percent of consumers expect to reduce their clothing consumption following the crisis." Despite reduction in apparel consumption, Hersan states that the future for resale will be bright with this new consumer mindset; "This will benefit resale massively as it's a more conscious way to enjoy fashion. It's really about buying less but buying better, investing in quality pieces that will stand the test of time."

Building Europe's major digital luxury resale platform was no easy feat, however, and Vestiaire must also focus on customer engagement. Hersan notes, "Now, more than ever, it's important to engage with our 10 million strong community and we take this seriously. Community engagement is key for Vestiaire and we often ask our community through our Instagram what they like to see in terms of content." This mode of engagement encourages consumers to share their opinions and facilitates an open relationship between the brand and the consumer. Hersan adds, "One thing we learnt during COVID is that they [the consumers] wanted to see more 'faces' of Vestiaire, so we profiled some members of our team who showcased their fabulous closets on Vestiaire, [and] #homemadebyVC was born!" While setting up a community within their followers, Vestiaire must also consider the various generational cohorts and the different ways in which they communicate.

I was interested to hear about the differences in the ways a Gen Z-er versus a Baby Boomer interacts with the vintage market, specifically within the luxury vintage realm. Hersan confirmed that "Gen Z and Millennials are definitely the audience demographics who are the leaders in driving the acceptance of pre-loved fashion, and we definitely see an uprising of the love for vintage items from this group." In deciphering the reason why these segments are the most active vintage community members, Hersan explains, "Social media is a huge driver for them, usually propelled by the celebrity and influencer effect."

To this extent, Hersan can even identify specific trends that have gained more popularity through social platforms such as Instagram, Twitter, Facebook, and now TikTok. Hersan says, "The return of vintage 'it' pieces like the Fendi Baguette [and] Dior Saddle has definitely brought more attention to the category and when celebrities and influencers are seen carrying these models, then it further fuels this younger generation's needs for them." What is also interesting about shopping differences between the generational cohorts is their consumer spending power. Hersan says, "Baby boomers are typically from an older, more mature age group so they can also afford higher price point vintage items, often classic, timeless items that you invest in and they retain value over time, such as vintage Rolexes or classic Birkins." A younger consumer does not have this much spending power, which therefore limits their consumption and also encourages savvier consumption practices that can stretch their dollars.

Hersan also notes that the younger cohorts are easily swayed toward trendier pieces—ones published on social media by various celebrities and influencers. In addition to generational differences in vintage hopping, there are also regional differences that Vestiaire must recognize and adjust to.

While Hersan is based in Vestiaire's Paris headquarters, she is readily able to pinpoint the differences between the European market that launched in 2009 and their market in APAC, or Asia-Pacific countries. The consumers in Hong Kong and Asia in general tend to purchase handbags as their entryway into luxury resale goods. Hersan attributes this behavior as being "most likely due to the fact that secondhand fashion has been around for longer in Europe, so people have long embraced pre-loved fashion including clothing as a category. In Asia, [when] we launched in Hong Kong over 3 years ago, we did see some resistance toward preloved fashion but we are seeing attitudes change, especially uplifted in Millennials and Gen Z." Hersan taps on a vital and fascinating topic here: the fact that vintage clothing is more normalized in Europe versus Asia since it has been around longer. Vestiaire was one of the first companies to bring luxury resale to the Asian market, which has a massive appetite for luxury goods.

Hersan also says that the United States actually is a part of Vestiaire's fastest growing markets throughout the world; the US alone counts for twice the amount of growth in new users and orders over the past year. She believes that many US consumers have changed their mindset in the wake of COVID-19 and are becoming increasingly passionate about sustainability and resale. In fact, Vestiaire launched direct shipping in the US earlier this year and has seen tremendous potential and growth. This growth has allowed Vestiaire's trusted and eligible sellers to ship directly to buyers, which in turn saves time and reduces the sellers' carbon footprint. Despite this option, more cautious buyers can still choose to have their items authenticated by Vestiaire's specialists.

Based on Vestiaire's great strides in the sustainability realm, I asked Hersan if luxury labels owe it to their consumers to have a completely sustainable development process. She enlightened me with her answer, stating, "I do think luxury labels have a part to play, and in fact, all businesses now need to be transparent about their actions. If they don't, then for sure consumers are asking more questions than before. But, more importantly, we all have a role to play. It's not down to one entity or company." While the importance of balance between the roles of the consumer and the producer is an excellent point, she also points a finger at bureaucracy; "Apart from businesses, I think that governments need to play a bigger role and implement more policies and rules that force people to take more action: recycle, ban bad textiles and chemicals in garment production, limit water usage, etc." We have come to a crossroads in the industry because everyone at each level of the industry has not played an active role. From governments to big business to consumers, everyone has taken a passive role that has led to overconsumption and extensive pollution that shrouds the current state of the industry.

It is truly up to everyone—consumers, retailers, and governments—to participate in active change. While small patterns in behavior can affect the whole, having these conversations about the fashion industry at large is more critical than ever.

In these discussions, we learn that there are other opportunities for change, growth, and innovation that will not only allow for more creativity but will also help the state of our planet. Hersan explains the noticeable shift Vestiaire has seen amongst its consumers in the United States by saying, "Sustainability resonates with environmental and socially conscious US consumers. This is, in fact, a global trend, and the international community is now more focused than ever on circularity issues." This is an incredible starting point for a vital market, but it isn't enough to simply have American consumers demanding more. Consumers all across the globe must step up to accept vintage goods and demand major supply chain changes and transparency. The opening of a new consumer mindset is an integral part of the future of fashion.

When asked what sustainability and the power of circularity means to her, Hersan gravitates toward the words 'movement' and 'new era.' These positive adjectives have something to promise consumers post-COVID-19: a new forefront for fashion. Through transparent companies, like Vestiaire, who recognize the needs of consumers and the planet, there is a bright new path for fashion to move forward. We, as consumers, must demand more from the brands we shop, but we also must recognize shopping the resale market as a conscious way to enjoy fashion. As Hersan puts it, "It's really about buying less but buying better, investing in quality pieces that will stand the test of time."

CHAPTER 7

THE VINTAGE MINDSET

———

Given the hundreds of pounds of clothing that Americans throw out each year, it is not hard to fathom that there are other ways of consumption that are actually better for us and for the environment. While everyone is not able to have their clothes custom-made by a tailor from high-quality textiles, we still have the ability to shop for vintage or second-hand clothing. Do those two terms not mean the same thing? Why does 'vintage' have a positive and trendy connotation while consumers shirk away from 'second-hand' and 'thrifted' shops?

To some people, used clothing has no particular meaning. It simply means used and is just another market in which you can search for new clothing, shoes, and accessories. In some minds, however, 'used' is a synonym for the old, the used, the worn out. These reactions to thrifted or second-hand items relate to the socioeconomic strata of the United States. Clothing has become a symbol of wealth for the upper middle class of Americans who have worked to afford new clothing and distance themselves from the not-so-fond memories of their hand-me-down clothing from older siblings and cousins. Clothing is also a symbol of wealth within the upper middle class of immigrants who have set up their lives and businesses in America. For these particular Americans, simply telling their friends at the next gathering that they're wearing a thrifted Milly cocktail dress would be an embarrassment. So why is it cool when the glamorous Instagram influencer wears the same thrifted Milly cocktail dress with a thrifted oversize leather blazer? Is there simply a difference because of age?

Well, not particularly. This influencer is roughly 30 years old and the same woman at the cocktail party is a forty-year-old suburban, well-dressed, and educated mother. Maybe it is truly a question of wealth, given that the influencer is not affluent but operates on a multitude of collaborations and clout to have access to a given number of expensive skincare and makeup products and a closet virtually full of new and vintage luxury goods. The suburban consumer, however, has access to luxury goods, high-grade skin treatments, and high-quality beauty products without a social media marketing campaign. She views the vintage mindset as something quirky but does not see it as an authentic means of consumption unless she finds a highly coveted vintage Chanel piece, which she would have her personal shopper locate for her.

The line between vintage being "cool" versus "old" is a fine one. I am not sure, however, if the solution is a simple matter of rebranding, since the vintage model does not belong to any one individual brand; instead, it involves every brand in every country across the globe.

It is interesting how some people mock vintage and second-hand clothes, calling them a "wannabe" symbol of wealth, since these used goods, whether luxury or not, are typically purchased at a fraction of the original retail price. Unfortunately, many people still hold this opinion despite the endorsements of fashion and beauty influencers across social platforms, who are just beginning to receive the acknowledgment they deserve within the fashion industry. They have been coined "influencers" for a reason—they influence the consumer purchasing decision by guiding consumers to certain products, brands, and even entire lifestyles.

The vintage market makes luxury goods seem more attainable for consumers because they don't have to purchase them at full price. However, many brands see the vintage market as a threat to their brand image and are worried about diminishing their exclusivity or coolness. Other brands recognize the massive influence of vintage shopping and know that it is the entryway for consumers who cannot afford the goods at the original retail price. Additionally, vintage can actually introduce consumers to a brand's luxury goods and encourage them to become loyal brand followers. Having access to a certain brand's vintage luxury goods may one day even inspire consumers to purchase new items at full price when they enter their professional, adult lives.

Some luxury brands such as Stella McCartney recognize these benefits and endorse or partner with vintage resellers such as the American game-changer, TheRealReal. Stella McCartney should be singled in out in particular because this brand champions ethical production, high-quality textiles, and a circular chain of consumption. This brand does not simply shout, "Sustainability!" from New York City rooftops, but rather embodies sustainability through its production, vision, and discernible efforts to make radical strides in an industry stuck in a gluttonous rut.[16] In January 2020, McCartney made the cover of American Vogue, who labeled her 'Fashion's Conscience' and recognized her as a champion of sustainable and ethical fashion business practices. McCartney is also a sustainability advisor on LVMH's executive committee and reports to Bernard Arnault, lending her expertise and passion to one of the industry's most powerful conglomerates.[17] She has also consulted with the United Nations on a sustainability charter. Despite her efforts, overall ethical change within the luxury realm has been slow, with Gucci just beginning to publicize their own efforts in 2020.

TheRealReal, an American luxury vintage reseller founded in 2011 by trailblazer Julie Wainwright, is exactly the kind of modern business model the industry needs. This e-commerce site, which now has opened brick-and-mortar stores across the country, bundles together a carefully curated selection of vintage designer goods that have been pre-approved, photographed, and categorized. TheRealReal essentially takes the anxiety out of hunting for designer goods and attempting to get the best deal possible. While this model is incredibly successful, it has also encountered fierce setbacks from individual brands such as Chanel, that do not approve of selling old product on the site. While Chanel believes selling

---

16   "About Stella McCartney" Stella McCartney, accessed March 19, 2020.

17   Ibid.

vintage items reduces the exclusivity of the brand, it actually increases their visibility and scope.

Resell platforms like TheRealReal, and its cooler European version, Vestiaire Collective, allow younger consumers—specifically those who do not have the same spending power as the core consumer of luxury brands—to access luxury goods through vintage pieces. The vintage model actually gives luxury brands more influence because it acts as an entryway into the exclusive aura of the luxury market. Young consumers become educated about a brand by following the development of a brand from the '70s, '80s, and '90s and all the way to the silhouettes on the runways today. In this way, the vintage model gives a consumer complete access to the brand's history through its previous collections, range of textiles, changes in logo, and essential items that remain as the backbone of the brand.

While the average consumer cannot afford, for example, the customized Louis Vuitton leather trunks that the brand's staple, they may be able to afford introductory items such as Vuitton's small leather goods. These items, however small, officially welcome them as members of the brand's community. With the recent rise in vintage resellers, this is the perfect example of products that can also be seen as the entryway to the brand as well. It is not a hinderance to the brand, but rather another opportunity to build brand loyalty and appreciation for high-quality textiles and artisan construction. It also encourages the circular model of consumption as consumers will invest in luxury products that they know they can someday resell. In this way, the handcrafted Italian leather tote lives for 100 years or more, the iconic Chanel suit goes from one generation to the next, and Balenciaga sneakers are valued as an everyday shoe, not just a pair designated for weekend strolls.

For the collective mindset to shift into appreciation for and knowledge of vintage items, I think it truly begins at the fashion education level. We, as fashion students and industry professionals, need to garner attention back to handmade clothing, shoes, and accessories. We are responsible for sharing with the public the importance of textiles, of artisans and craft, and of buying vintage and maintaining a circular mode of consumption. When vintage becomes not only cool and trendy, but also a societal norm is when we will see the beginnings of a shift. I personally take this special knowledge of vintage goods and share it with my mother, a member of Gen X and one the cohort's 82 million people in the United States who also share an aversion to vintage clothing. In order to create a shift in the older generation's mindset, there must be an increased awareness and popularity surrounding the vintage marketplace, which is what platforms such as The Vestiaire Collective aim to do.

I have thus far convinced her to resell her handbags, shoes, and denim. She then takes her profit and invests it in new products, whereas I would take her store credit and buy a different item in-store. Despite my efforts, I have yet to convince her to buy a vintage piece. She claims that she has just not found anything she likes, but I know it is because she is not fond of the idea of wearing someone else's clothes. One of my college friends, a finance major whose family is from Pakistan, agrees that her own mother shares the same viewpoint. Despite her mother's opinion, my friend states that she views vintage as being "similar to a piece of art—it always tells a story. It embodies the story of the previous owner, who they were, what they were doing when the item was worn, maybe the emotions they felt. Vintage clothes are much more than a piece of clothing, they're a collectible [item]."

SOLUTIONS: HOW TO BREAK THROUGH THE STEREO-TYPE OF VINTAGE

Whenever I consult my friend group and ask their opinions on vintage or used clothes, I am greeted with various forms of approval ranging from shrieks of delight to favorite garments being pulled out of closets to be admired. My friends range from ages 19 to 24, all well within the Gen Z bracket and demonstrative of the cohort's main qualities: independent, technologically fluent, and open-minded. We, collectively, are the most ethnically diverse and inclusive generation out of all cohorts, and our spending habits reflect our open minds and tech-savviness.

My friends shop online, on apps, in thrift stores, at Zara, and at luxury retailers. Some of them subscribe to rental services while others are designers or creatives and actually make most of their own clothing. One of the most interesting aspects of all of these different people with varying hobbies and lives is that none of them mind wearing a second-hand item. They all view such a garment as having a particular story attached to it and they all want you to inquire where they got their cool leather jacket, how they're wearing a different designer belt every day, or whether or not their Gucci bag is real so that they can tell you they swiped it at a vintage shop long ago on a quaint street in Florence. They want you to envy the story behind their finds and admire how they style their vintage pieces.

How they came across a luxury good—whether it was purchased new or thrifted—does not register to my friends as being a detail that they should hold back. My generation revels in the trendiness and cool factor attached to shopping second-hand. They especially love to go to these shops to find something particularly outrageous or unusual to wear to the next party or photoshoot for their blog, or just to browse for fun. In a time where everything is very uncertain and where there is so much noise in the market, my generation finds solace in the past rather than in the future. They browse the racks of endless possibility, of already tried and true styles, of garments that someone else wore when they met the love of their life to find their newest addition to their closet.

When I studied abroad, I lived in an adorable apartment in a very ideal location—above my favorite panino shop, a wonderful consignment shop, and a very bizarre furniture and antique shop. I could never go home without visiting each of them. Often times I would leave empty handed, but other times I would leave with armfuls of new finds. It was if I was hypnotized; I felt innately compelled to make these ritual rounds or I would feel uneasy. I had this ugly, itching feeling that something magical was sitting in the window display that changed every other day or tucked into some remote corner that I did not browse through adequately enough. My desperate search for an item I did not even know I was looking for was not solely confined to my block, since my apartment was very close to even more vintage shops, which I frequented often. I rifled through every rack, tried on every pair of shoes, touched every item. As I continuously conversed with the shop owners in Italian, they grew to appreciate my presence and would praise my choices or show me new things that I might like. These rituals and moments of deep human connection and appreciation for beautiful objects are vital to the process of vintage hunting.

The pure thrill of walking into the shop to discover something totally unknown to you is arguably the best part of the process. Bring a friend to go with you and find an amiable shop owner, and you have the perfect recipe for a successful vintage hunt, even if you don't leave with anything. I still recall a day I was feeling blue and decided to putz around in the shop below my apartment just to let my mind wander as I sifted through the beautiful things. That day I found a gorgeous pair of cream Ferragamo trousers in my size hiding behind other items on a wall. I immediately tried them on. The owner glanced over and—although she was with another customer–exclaimed that they fit me like a glove. I knew I had to have them.

I was not even close to being the only fashion student abroad who spent a majority of her time popping in and out of vintage shops and boutiques; my friend Larissa, who also spent three semesters studying fashion and art in Florence, says she can attribute roughly 75 percent of her wardrobe to vintage pieces she collected throughout her time in Florence. When I think about the sheer enjoyment that shopping for vintage pieces brings, I question why more consumers cannot hone in on this enthusiasm when they are also passionate about fashion and beauty. I started to wonder if this sentiment, often shared by older consumers like my mother and my friends' parents, isn't the result of a lack of interesting brick and mortar locations to draw consumers in to and change their minds.

In Florence, the vintage shops had interesting window displays that encouraged people to wander in and look through merchandise. In New York City, however, the vintage shops are often more hidden, do not put on a show, and the employees do not converse with you in the same way that the Italian shop owners will. TheRealReal also has a few brick and mortar locations in New York that lack imagination and take a certain nostalgia out of the hunt for something new and exciting.

The creative solution to these issues lies not only in shifting the consumer mindset and convincing consumers of the value of higher quality, long-term goods, but also in demonstrating that today's best dressed embrace the principle, "What's old is new." Today, with the impacts of COVID-19, the uncertainty about the future, and the bankruptcies of hundreds of brands, it is critical to adopt the vintage mindset.

The current consumers of vintage goods are divided, interestingly enough, between young trend setters and an older, more established consumer with more purchasing power. Despite the differences between these two consumer segments, they have much in common; both groups appreciate a vintage item because it has a story and they view them as a piece of art. Both of these segments are interested in circulating goods in the vintage economy, both by selling and buying the products. They look at a vintage collection as a way to elevate their style to the next level and to really experiment with their looks through colors, silhouettes, and new designers. By demonstrating the cool pieces they have found, whether through an online blog, an Instagram account, or another social media platform, even more people are exposed to this market.

Unfortunately, there has not been a widespread shift due to the negative connotations of vintage and the necessary skills needed to shop vintage; one who seeks vintage goods has to have a trained eye or must be well-informed of product before embarking a hunt. The slew of brands that one can find in a vintage shop—especially in a well-curated one or one in a metropolitan area—is endless. In some suburban and rural areas, on the other hand, there is not enough product. The vintage status remains truly in the hands of the beholden. The young creatives and older, polished fashionistas are the ones designated to set the trends and post the recommendations for the masses. It is not a simple persuasion, since it often takes the majority of consumers quite a while to catch up to early adopters of vintage fashion, but it can be done. The power of social media is not to be underestimated, as it is the singular tool to which basically everyone has access. Social media will lead consumers not only to the discovery of vintage mindset, but also to a whole new array of brands as well.

CHAPTER 8

SEMPRE AMICI

———

It's 7:00a.m. and his body is tense with anticipation for what he might find. An 18th century helmet? A pilot's jumpsuit? This is a typical morning for Danilo Ceri, owner of Ceri Vintage in the heart of the Oltrarno district,—Florence's creative and cultural hub. Ceri is a well-known figure in Florence not only for his impressive vintage collection but also for his welcoming personality and instant warmth that draws clients in as friends and costumers. When asked what his clients are like, Ceri answers simply and swiftly, stating, "Amici. Sempre amici," which means, "Friends. Always friends." Ceri's shop is run more like a museum rather than as a retail business. Friends and famous designers often stop by to chat, have a glass of wine, and admire pieces from various time periods.

Ceri often looks for articles that have a detail which totally draws in the eye. Whether it be a zipper, a pocket, or an interesting trim, he finds the items that have that little bit of spark to catch a designer looking for inspiration off-guard. When asked about his favorite pieces, however, Ceri responds without a doubt, "I like mostly military [garments] because from military you can do anything, and from non-military vintage pieces you cannot remake anything. And from the military [wear] you can do any collection. It can be elegant; it can be streetwear—you can do everything." Danilo Ceri's reflection on the malleability of military uniforms and the lure of no-name labels shows a striking truth about the shifting perspective of vintage and the state of the fashion industry today.

Danilo Ceri began going to markets to search for treasures when he was twelve years old, and from the very first military helmet he found to the vast collection he has acquired today, it is clear that Ceri has an eye for the unique and unusual. While his shop specializes in nineteenth century and World War II pieces, Ceri has amassed items ranging from the 15th century to the '90s, which has determined his rather exceptional customer base.

THE RISE OF ASIA
When asked which trend he prefers at the moment, Ceri cites emerging Japanese and Chinese designers. He says of their unique style, "I like the shape of the design even if it is extravagant. I like something like that. They pay attention to textiles, and I like to see and feel the wash of the dying, those that they make distressed, that kind of vintage look." What is most striking about Ceri's opinion on the rise of Asian designers and their consideration of textiles is the actual process of fabric development that has been around since the Yamato Period (c. 300-710 CE) in Japan. The art of Japanese textile production began with natural fibers from the likes of silk, hemp, ramie, cotton, and more. Indigenous techniques and external forces inspired such techniques, which

in turn fostered the technological advancements of the process. During the Yamato Period, textiles flourished mainly because the state supported weavers and artists, specifically in imperial workshops that even employed textile workers from mainland Asia.

The Japanese cultivation of textiles has created a niche in the market that is in fact openly recognizable and valuable within the industry today. Ceri notes excitedly, "Old style [is] in the sense of classic. If someone wants that, they go to their own private tailor and they do a *misura un abito* [size a suit or dress] because that is the only way to do the best." Although Italian tailors have been revered for their impeccable work for decades, it is a palpable change within the market today as the luxury Asian consumer base rises alongside the recognition of Japanese and Chinese designers and textile producers.

THE MOST VALUABLE ARTICLES

One day, a fashionable woman popped into Ceri's shop and said, "I have something vintage." Fascinated, he asked, "How vintage? Like 1950?" She replied, "Old." On the edge of his seat, Ceri asked, "1920? Beginning of 1900s?" She stood her ground by saying, "No, old." Ceri could barely contain his excitement now. "Fino ottocento [end of the 19th century]?" She casually responded, "No, più vecchio, primo ottocento [no, older, before the 18th century]." All Ceri could say was, "Wow, can I see?"

She complied and showed him a brocade waistcoat, riding coat, and a tricorne hat in the box. Ceri estimated the pieces were from around 1820 or the Napoleonic era, which dates to the 18th century. While he paid several thousand euros for the pieces, Ceri claims the value is much higher, especially since the items came from old relatives of the Granduke of Tuscany in Florence. While this may sound like an uncommon sale, it just all part of Ceri's daily job that puts him in contact with many rare and outstanding items from all points in time.

A TYPICAL DAY ON THE JOB

While Ceri owns and runs his archive, a typical day does not always begin at the shop, and is nothing like working at an office, he says. Some days, Ceri may arrive at a market by 7:00a.m. for the first picks. Other days, he must take care of the "new" old garments he recently purchased, which involves going to a dry cleaner and mending the items. He also speaks of the liveliness of the business behind curating the "new" old collection which he shows to designers who come in.

In the past, Ceri visited markets all over the world—from London to Paris to New York—to buy and sell as well as visit the cities. During his brief visit to New York for the La Tuta exhibition at Marist College, he happened to stumble upon a pop-up market. He says, "There was a vintage fair in Manhattan the other day, but nobody knew it here. I saw on Google. . .and I went after [the exhibition] and bought a couple of ethnic pieces." Ceri's line of work is restless, but he says, "The work is always fun. I look always for pieces—taste, a zipper, a pocket, a sleeve."

With the hopes of finding an extraordinary item, some of the most famous designers in the world enter Ceri's door for a unique taste of inspiration. It is no coincidence that the shop sits on the same street where the first recorded fashion show in 1951 by Giovanni Battista Giorgini occurred. It is also only a few steps away from Palazzo Pitti, the home of the famous Pitti Uomo exhibition for avant-garde men's fashion held bi-annually. Danilo Ceri's unique location and inherent talent to find the rare and remarkable items to inspire the world's creative geniuses is no small feat. Ceri knows that sometimes the key to an entire collection lies in the smallest detail, which is why he compares his archive to a museum rather than a shop.

CHAPTER 9

THE AGE OF THE AMATEUR

———

ABOUT

Li Edelkoort is a famous and well-respected Dutch trend fore-caster who has spoken about the dangerous business prac-tices of the fashion world. Before we encountered COVID-19, Edelkoort was leading discussions and proposing novel ideas in her articles, highlighting the damaged industry and call-ing for the renewal and reinvention of business practices. Her website reads, "As an intuitive thinker who travels the world studying the evolution of socio-cultural trends before shar-ing this information with her clients in industries as diverse as fashion, textiles, interiors, cars, cosmetics, retail and food. Under her Paris-based company *Trend Union*, Edelkoort creates trend books two or more years ahead that are tools used by strategists, designers and marketeers at international brands."[18] Trend forecasting is a unique branch within the fashion industry which acts similarly to Adam Smith's

———

18   "lidewij edelkoort" Lidewij Edelkoort, accessed March 20, 2020.

invisible hand within the economy. The hand of trend forecasting affects not only future trends but predicts consumer behavior patterns and emerging social, economic, technological, and other major global changes. Edelkoort believes reinvention is necessary to be consistent with today's reality and that both we and our environment desperately need a cultural agent of change within the fashion industry.

THE ANTI-FASHION MANIFESTO

Edelkoort's anti-fashion manifesto from late 2016 describes the future of fashion as she sees it across a variety of realms. In a lot of ways, this manifesto has come to fruition in 2020, with the onslaught of a global pandemic and rapidly changing consumer mindsets.[19] Edelkoort speaks of shifts that need to occur in order to improve the fashion industry, an industry she notes that, as a whole, has quite literally lost its ability to be avant-garde. As a result, other industries have filled that gap. When we consider how a variety of other sectors feed into the development of fashion, there should be little surprise at Edelkoort's words. Interestingly, they have actually come as quite a shock to leading industry professionals.

For instance, take the otherworldly success of the avocado, a fruit praised as a 'superfood' that has quite literally transformed Western diets. After the contingent success of the avocado in the food, wellness, and beauty industries, we saw

---

19   Robert Cordero, "Li Edelkoort: 'Fashion is Old Fashioned' Trend forecaster Li Edelkoort presented key excerpts from her 'Anti-Fashion' Manifesto, challenging an industry she described as 'no longer part of the avant-garde,'" *Business of Fashion,* December 5th, 2016.

the avocado influence fashion through a variety of prints, color schemes, and shapes. All it took was the tipping point of the avocado landing on breakfast menus, used as a main ingredient in pasta dishes at vegetarian restaurants, and featured in eye creams from brands like Kiehl's to see an avant-garde food effect fashion. The same can be said for a variety of trends across many industries, but the most important message from this claim is that fashion is no longer at the forefront of innovation and creativity. The industry has come to a massive standstill as a result of a lack of collaborative forces and the lack of an integrated, open source supply chain that serves a variety of brands and significantly cuts back on waste.

IN THE WAKE OF COVID-19

In her most recent podcast for Business of Fashion, Edelkoort has discussed her insistence upon the human and economic disasters that COVID-19 has brought upon the industry. The global pandemic has left no one unaffected and has wreaked havoc for global supply chains, small businesses, and the future of design and merchandising as we know it. Surprisingly, Edelkoort sees this virus as a saving grace for the planet and as a gift that has been bestowed upon the fashion industry's ambition and change. There will be few winners after this virus recedes, but those few surviving brands will be those that refused to remain tone deaf to the situation and that will provide ethically sourced, high-quality essential goods. There also will be a noticeable regression of demand for items that are non-essential; in fact, the way we categorize goods as essential and non-essential will completely change. Companies will be going bankrupt left and right as a direct result of their clients going bankrupt, which will lead to many job losses that will have a rippling effect on retail, fashion, and the economy as a whole for years to come.

While Edelkoort's podcast was eye-opening and in line with the major crisis brands face due to the pandemic, she was already predicting that these detrimental issues would eventually be brought to the forefront. In a *Business of Fashion* article from December of 2016, Edelkoort said, "How can a product that needs to be sown, grown, harvested, combed, spun, knitted, cut and stitched, finished, printed, labelled, packaged and transported cost a couple of Euros?"[20] Think about it. How can you justify the human capital it takes to plant, grow, and harvest cotton, which is then pulled and spun by machines into thread that then must be woven again with machines and human labor into a t-shirt available for you to buy in New York City? That does not sound like a $12 process, precisely because it is not. Somewhere along the way, the process of creating and manufacturing a garment has gone rogue. Somewhere along the way, people began to value a $6 t-shirt more than a $50 t-shirt that will actually last for years.

Edelkoort blames this variance upon the marketing machine and big business practices that have swallowed the creative process whole. In the same article she says, "It is, without doubt, the perversion of marketing that ultimately has helped

---

20 Robert Cordero, "Li Edelkoort: 'Fashion is Old Fashioned' Trend forecaster Li Edelkoort presented key excerpts from her 'Anti-Fashion' Manifesto, challenging an industry she described as 'no longer part of the avant-garde,'" *Business of Fashion,* December 5th, 2016.

kill the fashion industries. Initially invented to be a science, blending forecasting talent with market results to anchor strategies for the future, it has gradually become a network of fearful guardians of brands, slaves to financial institutions and hostages of shareholder interests, a group that long ago lost the autonomy to direct change. Marketing has taken over power within the major companies and is manipulating creation, production, presentation and sales."[21]

One of the most profound topics that Edelkoort speaks of is growing up in the 1950s, when products were of higher quality and were built to last. She predicts a return to these goods as consumers begin to demand more from the brands they seek out. They will also reduce their number of purchases, so each purchase must be an investment. When we think of an investment piece, we often consider a beautiful pair of black leather boots, a heavy wool jacket, or a black pantsuit—all items that will remain timeless and useful throughout one's life.

Fast fashion truly changed the nature of our wardrobes, and it did so on such a scale that it has created an even larger frenzy: an innate greed to constantly consume more. The absolute worst part of this business model is that these clothing and textiles will not remain in people's wardrobes forever. In fact, statistically speaking, the fast fashion industry manufactures clothing that remains in a person's closet for about year that

---

21   Robert Cordero, "Li Edelkoort: 'Fashion is Old Fashioned' Trend fore-caster Li Edelkoort presented key excerpts from her 'Anti-Fashion' Manifesto, challenging an industry she described as 'no longer part of the avant-garde,'" *Business of Fashion*, December 5th, 2016.

mostly goes unworn or is damaged due to cheap materials. This sector of the industry encourages constant newness and fuels the desire to be a part of the latest trends from the runways. After this pandemic, we will need to completely reset this collective mindset; there must be a collaborative effort to decide what is essential and what is not, to demand less and to take pleasure in how nice it is to have less. This pandemic has provided us with a true opportunity to address the nature in which we produce, dress, and consume.

THE RESULTS

This new collective mindset will shift into visible results through new and improved business models. The issue is not technology; the technology exists, but fashion companies at both the corporate and small business level do not utilize it or monetize it in the way they should… but this is all about to change. Every part of this industry post COVID-19 is going to become more human, more personalized, and more emotional. People are going to prefer word of mouth over direct mailings, digital samples will become more prevalent, and fashion shows are going to shrink to intimate gatherings. Every aspect of the industry is about to transform into something more intimate and manageable—something more collective that unites rather than excludes people.

Fashion shows will no longer be an exclusive production that thousands of people attend. There will no longer be tons of useless goodie bags and other wastes from traveling, production, and after parties. Fashion shows will evolve into something more artisanal and personal, and in turn, will actually favor the fashion designer. These shows—along with fashion as a whole— will revert to the very nature of design. Consumers will seek to find out exactly *how* a garment, shoe, or home accessory is designed, what materials they contain, and what functions they will serve.

Edelkoort suggests that this shift in mindset might expand on a larger scale to also reduce the number of companies seeking to replicate highly sought-after luxury items. Instead, she argues that they could combine design and production forces; by consolidating companies, product developers, sourcing, and manufacturing, the fashion industry could potentially create a universal hub that companies would approach to decide on a style to put into production, rather than having multiple companies traveling around the world seeking production and sourcing. Not only would this strategy consolidate production, but it would also reduce the amount of waste resulting from traveling and producing millions of samples that have to be approved. Fashion is a wasteful industry, not only for the excess of garments it produces, but also for the travel requirements and copious amount of goods entailed in marketing and PR events. Instead of seeking to target the masses via channels of communication and giveaways, there instead will be a return to person-to-person interaction.

There is no better retailer to exemplify this process than the institution of Bergdorf Goodman, a part of the Neiman Marcus group. Bergdorf's actually trains its sales personnel to acquire clients, get to know them personally, and carefully assess incoming product to curate a range of items that the client might want to see. Then, the salesperson calls the client to tell her about the new pantsuit that came in, the perfect dress for her niece's graduation, or the new Italian boot to supplement her winter wardrobe. This kind of intimate advertising that was once an industry staple is going to make a comeback precisely because it is built upon the values that will remerge in the wake of COVID-19. These values will be rooted in personalization, inclusivity, and festivity. People are going to be more interested in experiences and being brought together rather than concerned with constant, wasteful newness.

CHAPTER 10

INDIGO EXTRACTIONS

———

THE SITUATION

In the ever-changing landscape of retail, there is one keen idea that has risen to the top of everyone's radar in the retail sphere, from designers to corporate moguls. We must innovate to reduce fashion's waste. From the standpoint of a fashion merchandising student, I have also noticed a particularly strong thread of innovation among young aspiring designers, merchandisers, and fashion enthusiasts. Many students—not only those in fashion—have begun to take action across the globe to initiate sustainable and ethical change. In August of 2018, Swedish fifteen-year old Greta Thunberg led a school strike for climate change, which inspired a series of similar strikes in Italy as well as in other countries fueled by younger generations.[22] There is a global outcry for change, and this change must be woven into every single industry, from fashion to food to gas and oil, which remains the most pollutive industry in the world. Despite the crucial changes

———

22   Charlotte Alter, Suyin Haynes, and Justin Worland, "TIME 2019 Person of the Year," *TIME Magazine*, Dec. 23/Dec. 30 2019.

that need to be made, fashion programs have adapted just as slowly to these new concepts as the industry has at large. To truly understand and facilitate these changes, there has to be cross-disciplinary collaboration between fashion and other sectors such as science and technology. A greater knowledge of the scope of fashion and of the environment's largest problems is the starting point for all future innovation and new initiatives.

Isabel Holden is a passionate and vibrant 22-year-old design student at Marist College. She has realized the nature of fashion's greatest hurdle and has dedicated her fashion design studies to a cross-disciplinary training in chemistry to assist her in identifying cutting-edge dyeing techniques and other new strategies. In May 2019, Holden won the prestigious Council of Fashion Designers of America's (CFDA) Liz Claiborne Design Scholarship Award for her inventive and ethical dyeing techniques. Her award-winning collection and business plan initiated her into sustainable tactics and groundbreaking techniques within the industry. I sat down with her to discuss the concepts of sustainability in the fashion realm, possible alternate business models, and her eco-friendly career aspirations.

NOT JUST A FASHION STUDENT

A native of Hopkinton, Massachusetts, Isabel Holden is a trailblazer in her design class and has earned a slew of achievements and incredible internship experiences ranging from Milly to Abercrombie & Fitch. She won the Liz Claiborne Design Scholarship Award by designing a sustainable capsule collection of 12 looks as an inspiration for the Claiborne brand. She collaborated with Marist's chemistry program to extract indigo dye from old scraps, pieces, and pairs of denim and used it to dye new garments, a process that is extremely beneficial for the future of design and fabric dyeing modernization. Holden worked on refining this technique with denim design experts at Abercrombie during the summer of 2019 and began to re-dye virgin and eco-conscious textiles with indigo extracted from old denim for her senior design collection at Marist's Silver Needle Fashion Show in May 2020. Denim is extremely important to Holden's developments, and when asked what her favorite textile is, without a trace of hesitation, she says, "Denim. There is so much science and history behind it. You can trace the indigo dye process back to every single country and every single continent because of how it developed over time."

Holden is exuberant as she explains the levels of indigo found in denim and informs me that a lighter wash does not yield nearly as much as a dark wash. In addition, Holden clarifies that she still needs to identify a use for the leftover pieces unused in the dyeing process. She proposes new ideas such as packaging, visual merchandising, or grinding it down and re-spinning the fibers to make new textiles. Holden has hope, however, that this indigo extraction method can be applied on a large scale as a service for large corporations and small brands alike. However, the time required to perform the extraction would mean a fashion company would most likely need to employ an entire lab of green chemists to make the dye process efficient and profitable. This severely limits the ability of smaller businesses, designers, and other creatives to effectively implement the technology with which

Holden has been experimenting. Holden notes that a way to creatively combat this hurdle would be a to start a non-fashion business of green chemists who would implement the extraction process and bottle and package the indigo to sell to brands and designers. This strategy would largely reduce the economic costs of the time-consuming process of maintaining an in-house lab.

ON SUSTAINABILITY

When asked what sustainability means to her, Holden dives in, saying, "Sustainability truly becomes effective in the way we ourselves choose to define it and then put it into practice. I believe a lot of people tend to immediately associate the word, 'sustainability' with the environment, and that is the first problem. Sustainability is not about being afraid of what the future may hold for us in terms of natural resources, but instead, it's about appreciating and using what resources we already have, making wiser choices from both the consumer and retailer perspective, and coming up with new and innovative business models, all with the hope to find solutions to current day global issues." Holden pushes on, passionately insisting that we have to change the existing structure of the industry through the appreciation and utilization of the resources we already have. Holden also recognizes that these changes begin with the consumer and brand relationship, as the notion of sustainability is becoming less of a taboo subject amongst consumers. Holden says, "It's a legitimate thing now [the brand image of sustainability], and it is important that the consumer is educated and people recognize which brands have ethical practices in place. It's critical that consumers not educated in the practices of the fashion industry understand that the brands they have been shopping are not financially doing well for a reason. People have migrated away from these mass retailers based on their values, their business models, and how they treat their workers."

Holden has a vast knowledge of sustainable tactics, which she attributes to the major research endeavor behind the business plan she created for the Liz Claiborne scholarship. Through this extensive research, she discovered brands who inspired the sustainable approaches within her design processes. Some pre-existing direct-to-consumer brands that aim to reach Gen Z-ers from an ethical standpoint are Patagonia, a longstanding brand known for repurposing old products, and Everlane, a relatively new brand with a focus on radical transparency. Holden admires these brands and insisted upon incorporating actual collaboration between science, fashion, and ethical production methods into her business model as well. She cites this cohesiveness between fashion design and science or technology as her primary reason for initiating a collaboration with the chemistry program at Marist College. She also argues that we must utilize tactics across all industries because the notion of sustainability is not only a fashion business model crisis.

Despite being a visionary in the design realm, Holden is not naïve, recognizing that there is no direct way for the fashion industry to become completely sustainable. Instead, there must be a slow and steady push for brands to change their ways. She sees the fashion industry as very black and white; "There are those [brands] beginning with a sustainable ethos and then there are those with a fast fashion focus who need to revisit their roots, brand image, brand values, and ethics to find places to truly jumpstart change. Until there is a major awakening amongst consumers and a deeper understanding of real sustainable practices versus greenwashing marketing techniques, there will always be a consumer for fast fashion." Holden believes we all have an inherent need for new things, but brands need to fully grasp and re-approach the psychology of the consumer's desire for newness in order to succeed in the fashion industry moving forward post COVID-19.

It is important to note that the rise of fast fashion has allowed brands to bring constant newness into their retail stores by unhealthy measures. Copying a couture design seen on the runways of Gucci, Dior, or Valentino and producing a cheap reproduction to sell at a mass retailer such as Zara within a few weeks encourages poor labor practices, pollution, and textile waste. Consumers all too often toss out a garment they purchased that is no longer on trend or that has literally fallen apart due to poor construction. This vicious cycle not only contributes to the planet's environmental issues but also reduces the value of true craftsmanship and the creative ability of designers.

POST-COLLEGE

Since graduating in May 2020, during the height of the COVID-19 outbreak and into a terrible job market, Isabel Holden has channeled her creative energy into pursuing freelance opportunities. One of these opportunities has led her to directly help the front-line workers of the outbreak; over the summer after graduating, Holden collaborated with a textile engineering company to design several disposable hospital gown prototypes that will be sold to certain hospitals and nursing homes across the United States. Her design is not only going to help workers in the fight against the pandemic but will also provide jobs; laborers in North Carolina, Mexico, and the Czech Republic will be producing her design. As of July 2020, over 10,000 gowns have already been produced.

Holden has also been working on selling her own personalized masks for her clients. Besides selling them directly from her Instagram shop, @artbyisabelholden, she also sells masks at two boutiques: Artichoke in Orleans, Massachusetts and Cinnamon Rainbows Surf Co. in Hampton, New Hampshire. Holden says of selling locally, "I want to sell via small businesses within my area and beyond as well to support them because it helps me make connections at a more personal level. I really get to know the owners, the customers, and it makes me feel more connected to those who support me." By the summer of 2020, Holden had sold over 300 masks made from scraps and leftover pieces of fabric from her design school work.

This particular mindset from young designers could potentially change the nature of the industry; fashion is returning to the local as more and more creatives are going to school and then setting up their businesses in their hometown and sourcing local talent in the area. Holden even acknowledges, "It's also important because small businesses are likely thinking about sustainability without even knowing it. I know the retail shop [Artichoke] I worked for uses recycled fabric to wrap hangers, reuses materials for shipping, and does everything in their power to think more consciously about how they can use sustainable tactics to save money and [their own] resources."

Going forward, Isabel Holden plans to keep producing handmade masks while pursuing a full-time career in textile innovation and development and sustainable design in New York City. Holden has always wanted to work in New York ever since she grew up visiting the city for inspiration and adventures. Holden notes that the city has been a constant source of inspiration "for its diversity, inclusivity, and chaos that fuels a designer's mind and creative ambitions."

CHAPTER 11

KEEP YOUR CADENCE

—

Have you ever thought about what actually happens to all of the plastic bottles that we recycle? The age of convenience demands products that can readily assist us in our highly mobile lives. Stephanie Hon, entrepreneur and founder of Cadence, recognized this problem long before all of us as a crucial day-to-day dilemma during a camping trip. As she was traversing through a magnificent forest carrying single use products that would end up in a landfill, she simply could not justify the matter any longer. After the trip, Hon set out to create a product—the kind of product that could evolve into a collection and maybe even change the way people move entirely.

I spoke with Stephanie Hon about her new company, founded with a sustainable ethos and reusable product line. The capsule bounces across the website boasting its design that allows one to move their: sunscreen, makeup remover, toothpaste, eye serum, aftershave, supplements, conditioner, retinol, Q-tips, body scrub, contact solution, vitamin-c serum, hair mask, face peel, mouth wash, and exfoliating mask. The product is a leakproof, sustainable, and personalized refillable capsule. It sounded like the exact product that was missing from my life as I lugged my shampoo and hair products in Ziploc bags across Europe during my freshman year of college.

At the time I was able to chat with Hon in Fall of 2019, the product was not yet released, but as of January 2020, Cadence has launched their first exciting product segment belonging to a series called: the capsule. The capsule is marketed as "the perfect way to bring your supplements, serum, and small jewelry with you on-the-move for everything from day-to-day to weekend adventures. It's pretty enough to put on your desk, but strong enough to be tossed around in your gym bag." Even more noteworthy, however, is the brand ethos.

Cadence is based in Hon's personal ideology in which she values bringing people together to complete projects together. Hon has always been fascinated with everything having a place, and a quality product. She noticed a problem and was already her own customer when she set out to create a collection of reusable travel containers to take on the go with her. She was on a hiking trip feeling cluttered and overwhelmed when she noticed all the women around her in the bathroom with clunky bottles and plastic bags as well.

Hon now has five different designs in the works, all are hexagonal and magnetic so they fit together as a unit to move with you rather than hindering your movement. Essentially, she has created the ultimate travel companion for everyday life on the go. Imagine a system as tall as your phone, a combination of hexagonal containers that each are extremely different, some with pumps and others where the bottom part unscrews, and another version in which there is a pump both on the top and bottom for more viscous serums and retinol. While Hon created a variety of designs, they all look the same on the outside, but internally they are different. Hon says that, "[Cadence] is not a travel company, but a movement company." This nuance between travel and movement is vital to the core of her business since new generational cohorts are rarely in one place. Simply branding her company as 'travel' oriented would be limiting as Hon aims to target the broader needs of consumer lifestyles that are increasingly on the move each and every day rather than for a specific vacation or holiday weekend.

The digital era has ushered in an age of constant movement, and there is not a huge product market that caters to this special need. Consumers not only need products for traveling, but also for their urban, day-to-day lives that take them from home to the gym to work to dinner and wherever else they may end up in a single day.

When asked what the word 'sustainability' means to her, Hon answers honestly, "lots of things, from a company perspective- how can we live within the realities of what we know? We know consumers want to be sustainable—it sounds really nice to them, but at the end of the day they will choose what is convenient. As a business, how can we know we are doing what is the very best for the world?" This is the very same reason that Cadence exists, refillable personal care products are designed for those consumers who want their own shampoo and makeup but do not have the means to bring their products with them. Hon also points out that we need to build sustainable packing solutions for a life on the move.

It is not simply enough to create an ethical product—the packaging also needs to be thought out. Hon elaborates on this eco-friendly notion, "We are going as far as we can. We have to push ourselves and innovate, such as open source technology so fashion brands can use them as well- make it available for other startups. Competition is good, but in this realm, it shouldn't be this way as a business owner, we need to do our best to create solutions for consumers—not changing their habits, creating around their habits."

The consumer Hon is designing for is the modern one—a consumer that is urban, moving around, and looking to foster an ethical lifestyle. People rarely stay in one place anymore, and even in a city, besides moving apartments or into a home, they move everyday within their lifestyles. Just as luggage has gone through a miniaturization process- from hefty leather trunks to personalized, compact four-wheel suitcases, it is time that our products become transportable as well. From moving to work and the gym to home again, or away for the weekend, or a longer trip overseas, the modern consumer needs to be able to take their life with them, and this involves creating sustainable packaging solutions across the board, not just in terms of a lightweight suitcase. From a fashion perspective, this transformation of life is extremely relevant as well since the way we dress has changed too. Fueled by the pandemic and switch to working from home, many consumers have now completely transformed their wardrobe to a more comfortable, 'athleisure' style of dress. People have realized that working from home allows for greater flexibility, which in turn has a fueled a mass exodus from cities to the countryside. With more people moving around and renting homes in various locations for brief periods of time, a product like Hon's has the opportunity to become a staple item in this new human lifestyle.

Hon works with Envision plastics, which employs locals in high-risk areas near beaches to collect the plastic off those beaches to create new products. By utilizing this business, Cadence is essentially rebuilding a product from already existing materials and supporting the U.S. economy at the same time. While this sounds like a fabulous solution that more companies should be seeking, it was actually quite difficult to find a company with which to work. She cited hours of research and phone calls since sustainable ocean plastic companies only want to work with conglomerates—not start-ups who actually have the ability to make a difference from day one.

Hon also notes that post-consumer plastic that is uncolored is basically non-existent, which marks another obstacle Cadence had to overcome in finding a technique to ethically dye the plastic to a color(s) that would please consumers. This is an important detail that many innovative entrepreneurs and small businesses face in the realm of sustainable production, whether the product is clothing, shoes, or reusable containers. The eco-friendly resources and connections available in the marketplace are not only expensive, but difficult to implement for a variety of reasons. For a brand like Cadence, the struggle comes in finding companies willing to fulfill smaller orders when they are used to large contracts, for a company like Aèropostale for example, the hardship comes in shifting to eco-friendly textiles which raises retail prices, and then persuading consumers to pay the upcharge by educating them on denim spun from ethically sourced cotton.

As the fashion industry struggles to adapt in the wake of the havoc caused by COVID-19, the brands and innovative leaders that were making great strides in creating compelling brand narratives and pursuing ethical standards of production and selling will be the ones to survive in the new fashion landscape. Stephanie Hon is one of the trailblazers creating a brand that not only solves a need in the urban marketplace, but also sets the new norm for brands. Cadence is founded upon transparent brand values in line with high-quality, ethically produced, and centered around a community of like-minded consumers. Hon defines her mission as, "[a] brand that builds intuitive solutions for the modern on the go consumer." Brands that focus on consumer needs while also creating a platform that encourages interaction will succeed, because they are truly aware that the new consumer is not simply just looking to buy a product, but is invested in their purchase—they are concerned about where the product is made, who is making it, and why they should buy small instead of searching for a cheaper supplement form a mass retailer.

Hon's brand mission and ethos, along with her product, is in line with new consumer values and encourages other brands to follow suit. In a pollutive industry that is largely focused on profit and reproduction, it is refreshing to interact with a brand that is making life easier for its consumer and is benefitting the environment by finding alternate, modern solutions for waste material that is vastly underutilized. It is Hon's pioneering efforts to find a technique to dye plastics that will change the nature of the industry bit by bit. She discussed how difficult it was to find companies that want to work with a smaller brand, how difficult it is to institute such ethical standards. Post COVID-19, I hope that more companies will be open to working with smaller brands and passionate entrepreneurs to execute innovative solutions to fashion's greatest waste problems.

CHAPTER 12

IF YOU CAN WEAR IT, I CAN EMBROIDER IT

———

Entrepreneurs like Steph Hon are making seismic changes in the innovation sphere of consumer goods, and there are also creative minds within the fashion industry that are stretching the lifecycle of product in new ways. In addition to buying vintage, consumers could also look to other retail outlets powered by artists and designers who decided to break off from the corporate machine and initiate their own sustainable principles and new, and higher ethical standards. The entrepreneurial mindset is an important asset within the industry, since it truly gives you the ability to be adaptable, ready to embrace change, and determined to leave your mark.

Marist College's fashion design program gives students the opportunity to pursue their creativity while encouraging industry ethics through coursework revolving around textiles, sustainability, and the development of a senior collection. I met Marist Fashion Design alumna, Morgan Powers, through a speaker at the fashion program's annual brunch, a wonderful networking and learning opportunity for students.

Marist Fashion's brunch gave me the exciting opportunity to speak with Powers, founder of her own brand, MPUSA, and well-versed apparel designer with over 7 years of industry experience in developing ready-to-wear, swimwear, and everything in between. Her time in the corporate design sector led her to start her own company and create custom upcycled garments for clients. Powers is passionate about sustainability and says that her business originally "began as a creative outlet for me and has grown into a successful and environmentally friendly side hustle."

Powers originally began her career at Mara Hoffman, a womenswear label devoted to transparency and sustainability, where her first interests in sustainability arose. She has always been into upcycling, also known as creative reuse, which is the process of transforming waste and by-products into new textiles or products of higher quality. This process helps reduce the fashion industry's environmental impact, although it is not a common practice. At Hoffman, however, Powers became more passionate about reducing textile waste and using less plastic—all groundbreaking initiatives that are in line with the label's core values.

Meanwhile, on the side, Powers was embroidering on scrap fabric and eventually on her own custom-made pieces for herself, her friends, and her clientele. The development of her brand has taken time, and she has learned about the complications associated with upcycling, which is not so simple to initiate within small or large brands due to the extensive knowledge of materials and ethical deconstruction. Powers notes that she eventually wants to grow her business from custom, hand-embroidered denim jackets and other requests into her own ready-to-wear pieces.

When asked what the word 'sustainability' means to her, Powers answered, "Doing things that will last, because our resources are not infinite." She speaks positively of the textile TENCEL™, which is a regenerative fabric similar in feel to rayon and Jungmaven, a brand that makes all of its products from hemp, the most renewable fabric available on the market today. TENCEL™ uses raw wood to make its Lyocell and Modal fibers environmentally responsible; they are both compostable and biodegradable. In addition, these fibers are soft on the skin and are versatile in combination with a variety of textiles to produce sustainable product.[23] Many brands already use these sustainable fibers, but it is not common enough throughout the industry to demonstrate a massive change yet. This is partially due to cost and time; as discussed in Isabel Holden's efforts with indigo extraction, these natural and renewable processes are lengthy and require significant effort and commitment. The brands that can incorporate environmentally responsible fabrics into their collections tend to be on the higher end, since they can either absorb the extra costs required to make the garments or make up for the extra amounts with high retail prices.

Morgan Powers also praises the work Patagonia has initiated through their WornWear program. They send clothes out

---

23 "about TENCEL™ fibers," TENCEL™, accessed November 25, 2019.

and bring in new ones to re-sell on their website.[24] While WornWear does not donate to a particular charity, Patagonia as a brand is making great strides in identifying and practicing the process of reusing, repairing, and recycling a used garment. The WornWear site boasts an interesting statistic on its front page: "Buying a used garment extends its life on average by 2.2 years, which reduces its carbon, waste and water footprint by 73 percent."[25]

While some brands like Patagonia are actually putting in the work to become more sustainable, other brands use sustainability as an advertising ploy. Powers states, "People might say jeans are sustainable because they use less water, but that doesn't necessarily imply sustainability. What about the cotton? How is that grown?" The term, "greenwashing," is used to describe how sustainability has lost meaning due to overuse and misuse in the industry through complicated marketing efforts to create an ethical brand image without actually addressing actual problems.

Powers practices what she preaches. She works with her customers through her website and Instagram account, offering a variety of services from painting and embroidering to bringing a customer's full vision to life with their choice of material. Powers typically works with denim and other light or medium weight woven fabrics and takes on projects involving a variety of vintage apparel items. She takes note of her skills on her website, emphasizing, "If you can wear it, I can embroider, sequin, paint, and bedazzle it. My skill

---

24 "WornWear - FAQ," Patagonia WornWear, accessed November 25, 2019.

25 Ibid.

set is not limited to clothing—I also work on home decor items and accessories." She gains new customers through her Instagram or word-of-mouth recommendations and works directly with her clients. She typically uses her own vintage apparel for projects but will also accept a customer's own apparel that they want transformed. By using apparel that she has thrifted or dead stock fabric, she eliminates the need for new material and adds to the circular economy of repurposing previously existing material and product.

Powers is a creative mind through and through. She believes that the clothes we wear reflect what is inside of us. Of her own style, she says she is "always in a print or something loud. There are definitely many people who do that [dress to reflect their personality], but not everyone does it to express themselves. Some dress for others." Powers has demonstrated the ability to create a business that not only has an ethical mission statement but is also truly rooted in ethics; she sources sustainable base materials solely from vintage items or scrap fabrics. She scours eBay, Poshmark, and thrift stores to find "new" old materials to work with and repurpose into a stunning denim jacket that is completely one of a kind. While Powers' dedication to an environmentally friendly business model is easier to carry out on a small scale, it still takes motivation; designers like Powers must spend time searching for the right materials to start with rather than ordering brand new fabric straight to her door.

Time consumption is a massive part of running an ethical business model, but it is also true that larger brands—ones that Powers favors such as Mara Hoffman and Reformation—have the capital to invest into ethical sourcing, production, and environmentally-friendly textiles. There is one catch, however, in designing for large brands, sustainable or not: they require a designer to execute the brand's vision. In fact, this is the exact reason Morgan Powers decided to kickstart her own brand. She wanted to breathe new life into clothes that already exist. Powers questions how fulfilling it is to bring more clothing into the world when there are already so many beautiful pieces that can be reimagined through her own design, artwork, and creativity.

Morgan Power's idea for her brand not only came from her talent in design, but also from her mission to preserve our planet and make it an amazing place for future generations. However, it is not up to one person to create a better planet for us all; collectively, we must institute sustainable sourcing initiatives, from locating eco-friendly base materials to reusing indigo dye extracted from used denim scraps. It is up to brands to recognize the sheer amount of pollution the fashion industry creates with every step of the production process. Consumer expectations for low prices and constant newness drive these unsustainable methods, to which COVID-19 has drawn unprecedented attention. Now, brands must re-align with consumer values that revolve around quality, repurposing, and ethical production.

Consumers are beginning to demand more, and these demands will cause shifts that are absolutely necessary for the fashion industry. They will ignite changes in brand missions, brand identities, and methods of production. Just as Morgan Powers recognized a dire need in the industry and set off to create her own brand to address the root of the problem, large brands will have to follow suit to maintain relevancy within a new wave of consumerism.

CONCLUSION

As I gauge the state of world affairs and prepare to launch myself into the professional world, I see a future that looks incredibly different from the world we know today. We have almost made it to the end of 2020, and the fashion, hospitality, and restaurant industries have all but unraveled in the wake of COVID-19. Legacy retailers are merging or filing for bankruptcy, small boutiques are shuttering their doors, mass consumer brands are offering heavy discounts, luxury brands have cancelled entire collections, and most product is sitting in the midst of the supply chain during its designated selling season. At the base of it all, fashion students are adjusting to a vastly different campus life, which has yet to fully adapt to students' needs. As schools implement strict regulations to slow the spread of COVID-19, they also must consider the tools and experiences students will need in a floundering industry, such as increased writing skills, entrepreneurial training, and an overall understanding of the current marketplace. Moving forward, the only brands that will survive are those with relevant products and excellent communication skills for interacting with consumers across a variety of platforms.

Take the letter from Marcus Wainwright, founder of New York label Rag & Bone, for example. In his letter, Wainwright writes, "The time for buying stuff for the sake of it is over. I, for one, am buying only things that I need, or things that mean something to me, that are properly made and that will last, and for me at least, sometimes a damn good t-shirt can make me feel a whole lot better than a disposable one."[26] Wainwright's letter is a strategic corporate attempt to maintain an inclusive community feeling and remain in touch with consumer sentiment in difficult times. His words certainly ring true; it is simply not justifiable for us to consume without a second thought anymore because the implications behind purchasing new product, season after season, is detrimental not only to ourselves but also to the planet. As Wainwright acknowledged in his letter, we must return to buying products that not only mean something to us but are also built to last.

In the '50s and '60s, a huge percentage of clothing was still manufactured in the United States, which provided jobs for factory workers, tailors, designers, and more. Goods were American-made, and Americans like my Sicilian grandfather were proud of this production and of purchasing American-made goods. There was a certain pride in dressing well and investing in high-quality garments. Unlike today, there was not a constant need for newness—just a need for duration and timelessness. These two concepts do not exist in the fashion industry today, at least not like they did in the '50s, '60s, or even '70s in America. While it is partially a matter

---

26   Marcus Wainwright, Rag & Bone, "A Message From Our Founder," Accessed March 2020.

of globalization, the largest step we can collectively take as consumers is redefining the principles of fashion that we all share. Once consumers decide to shift their ideas and make a change, we will begin to see active changes within the industry.

I recently spent a Sunday in Williamsburg, Brooklyn with some friends exploring the vintage markets and lunching outside. Despite the mass exodus from the city due to COVID-19, Brooklyn has remained quite busy in comparison to Manhattan. The young population has worked around the new restrictions to ensure the health and safety of the community while also trying to resume some sense of normalcy. Stores have moved racks of clothing outside while restaurants have taken over the streets with outdoor patios. While roaming around Brooklyn, I found a men's vintage shop that had gorgeous stacks of clothing and displays of carefully curated outfits.

I wandered in to get a better look and was greeted by a very polite and immaculately dressed salesman who brought down a beautiful indigo French chore jacket from the 1960s that I was admiring. Although it had a small hole and a paint stain, it was sturdy and had large pockets, just like the ones I had seen in Paris years ago and haven't found since. When I told him I wanted to purchase it to wear with my cream-colored sweatshirt underneath, he led me to a corner of neatly piled thick, white sweatshirts from the '70s and '80s with tags ranging from $80 to $90. I touched one heavy sweatshirt to examine the label and was shocked to find a Champion tag on such a well-constructed sweatshirt. The salesman saw my surprised face and offered an alternate pile of white sweatshirts from the '50s and '60s that were equally heavy and well-made. These ones had tags ranging from $120 to $150. A friend who was with me shuddered at the prices, but when I called her over to feel the material, she couldn't believe it. I told her that these were expensive because they were American-made in the '50 and '60s with much better cotton fibers and none of the artificial blends found in our sweatshirts today.

If we were to take these the concepts of quality and timelessness and apply them to the fashion industry today, it would more than resonate with consumers. The entire fashion industry needs to rebrand its image in order to make the change into a high-quality retail environment and a better world for all of us. This does not mean consumption would come to a halt or that we would all begin dressing in a utilitarian style; instead, as Wainwright stated, it would mean investing in good t-shirts that are not only cool and well-made but that also make us feel proud to wear. A single, high-quality t-shirt is more valuable than a stack of 20 cheap t-shirts from the likes of Primark which practically disintegrate after a few wears and washes.

On a larger scale, the future of retailing will bring many changes to our methods of shopping and to the products we actually consume as well. My grandparents—members of the Silent Generation—collected and analyzed the weekly flyers from Market to decide what meat they would purchase, and which non-perishable goods such as canned tomatoes, steak sauce, and pasta they could add to their stockpile. All of their cabinets were labeled and stocked accordingly with dry goods, just in case of an emergency.

Consider Millennials shopping this way. It would never happen. My 28-year-old Millennial cousin goes to her local grocery store several times during the week. She buys her wine from a small boutique and has a wine subscription service. Her Millennial boyfriend orders their groceries and household items through an app that pays a shopper go to multiple stores to pick up the things they need. As someone on the cusp of Gen-Z and Millennials, I either order through a farm to table delivery box that brings me products from the Hudson Valley, or I stop into the market a few times throughout the week, picking things up as I need them. A weekly vegetarian produce box that I customize also arrives at my door along with any additional pantry items I might need from local producers, such as Hudson Valley yogurt, freshly baked sourdough, or canned beans and bags of lentils. My mother, a Gen X-er and my father, a Baby Boomer, take bi-weekly trips to Market Basket or Stop & Shop. I think the way my family members of various generations shop is largely representative of the generational cohorts in urban, middle-class American families. I also think this is all about to change.

Amazon has established itself as a powerhouse in the e-commerce sector in America and will remain there as demand surges. However, they have had numerous problems such as workers contracting COVID-19 in over 500 of their warehouses and not paying their workers for sick leave. Despite Amazon's issues, people are still ordering essential and non-essential goods from the e-retailer as it looks to move into the luxury consumer segment since brands going bankrupt and seeking a sale. Mass retailers such as Gap are suffering and must offer heavy discounts while small boutiques shutter and luxury collections and fashion shows are canceled. Young designers have nowhere to showcase their designs as wholesale business is disrupted and brick-and-mortar retailers continue to struggle. I think the future of retail and shopping will revolve around online subscriptions and rental and subscription business models like Rent the Runway for fashion and Trade Coffee and Brightland Olive Oil in the grocery sphere. Specialty food boxes crafted by companies that use local products from farms and boast fresh produce will replace trips to the market and grocery store, as these boxes can be delivered directly to your door.

I believe that due to social, economic, political, and ethical standards, people will stop consuming so frivolously post COVID-19. In the future of retail, people will only purchase essential goods like a few pairs of jeans, several well-made t-shirts, and a wool coat and will subscribe to a rental clothing company to supplement their closet with everything else they might need. For women, that may be a formal dress to wear to a wedding or a colorful jacket just for brunch with the girls. For men, that could be a tuxedo for a black-tie event or a sleek brown suede jacket to wear on a trip to Europe. People will also use their rental service to try out fashion items they would not necessarily pay for but would like to try out, nonetheless. In terms of shopping for food and household items, I also think people will start using the subscription model more frequently.

When I returned home from college, I ordered my family groceries on Amazon and had them delivered to our door. I also signed up for a grocery box delivery service. My best friend has a coffee subscription and sent me a discount code to join and have my favorite roasts automatically shipped to me on a recurring basis. I know people who also use olive oil, wine, and pet subscription services. When global pandemics or other extenuating circumstances arise, the need to have items delivered to us to reduce our contact with people will only increase. The option to have items personalized and delivered will drive businesses. During COVID-19, people have gone to the stores, seen empty shelves, and become scared to be in public. As a result, Amazon is performing extraordinarily well due to its efficient shipping and delivery services. Post COVID-19, I don't see the state of grocery shopping or normal retail shopping changing for quite some time. There will continue to be shortages and fewer people in-store. More consumers will sign up for at-home delivery subscriptions which allow a contactless transaction.

Above all, it is important to maintain a sense of focus and purpose in the new age of retail. Brand values are integral and are the key to obtaining sustainability and running a long-term business operation. In the post COVID-19 era consumers will question brands and their ethos with, "Why does your brand matter? and What are you doing differently?" The values of a brand must match the same internal values that consumers now have in light of today's circumstances. The industry needs to be reinvigorated by beauty, authenticity, and innovation. Consumers must demand quality and transparency from brands, which in turn will help reduce the number of fast fashion conglomerates that oversaturate the market today.

Although these companies have taken a hard hit during the pandemic, in an article from the October 2020 edition of American Vogue, Maya Singer says that "Zara alone produces about 450 million garments each year. . . *What are we going to do with all this stuff?*" [27] Singer poses a wonderful question for us all: if we collectively don't make a change, where are the millions of pounds of clothing going to go? Singer's next thought actually contributes to the ethos of this book:

"Secondhand shopping is one answer. Gen Z'ers are flocking to apps like Depop that lets them thrift directly from peers' closets, and sources from a 2019 McKinsey report predict that the resale market a decade from now could be larger than that of fast fashion—a cheering prospect if you fret about the millions of tons of apparel dumped in landfills annually. Other answers include upcycling—retrieving fibers from fabrics to make new ones—and 'regenerating,' as Marine Serre terms her innovative method of re-crafting old garments and textiles." [28]

The COVID-19 pandemic has quite literally brushed the dust off of important conversations that have long been overdue in the fashion realm. Now, the most pressing issues we face in the industry have been brought to the forefront. Consumers are becoming aware of their choices and demanding more, which is a major step in returning to the original reasons why

27 Maya Singer, "Can Fashion Be Political? Always- but now more than ever. As the world undergoes a radical transformation, Maya Singer looks at how the industry is reckoning with momentous and much-needed change," *Vogue,* October 2020, 124.

28 Maya Singer, "Can Fashion Be Political? Always- but now more than ever. As the world undergoes a radical transformation, Maya Singer looks at how the industry is reckoning with momentous and much-needed change," *Vogue,* October 2020, 124.

we love and participate in fashion: because it is a reflection of who we are.

It used to be about quality, taste, and the lifespan of a garment, but we have been enveloped by greed, big business, technology, and new ways of living. Suddenly, how long a sweater lasts does not matter because you can walk into any store and buy a new one for just $20. This mentality must change. Our livelihood depends on it, future generations depend on it, and our planet depends on it. We must evolve in the direction of creative change, whether that shift means more people shopping second-hand, more brands creatively marketing high-quality garments, or both. Our planet is crying for change. The pandemic, as tragic and transformative as it may be, has started this necessary change. All we have is the future.

APPENDIX

———

PREFACE

CHAPTER 1

Edelkoort, Li. "The BoF Podcast: Li Edelkoort Says the Corona-virus Is a Representation of our Conscience." March 27, 2020. In *Special Edition Inside Fashion*. Produced by BOF TEAM. Podcast, MP3 audio. https://www.businessoffashion.com/articles/podcasts/the-bof-podcast-li-edelkoort-on-how-covid-19-is-ushering-in-the-age-of-the-amateur.

Foussianes, Chloe. "What Is Fast Fashion, and Why Is Everyone Talking About It?" Town & Country, January 17, 2020. https://www.townandcountrymag.com/style/fashion-trends/a30361609/what-is-fast-fashion/.

Markovich, Jeremy. "At Hudson's Hill, Denim is The Deepest Blue." *Our State*, August 5, 2015. https://www.ourstate.com/at-hudsons-hill-denim-is-the-deepest-blue/.

Sherman, Lauren. "Unravelling the Myth of 'Made in America'."
Business of Fashion, November 7, 2016. https://www.busines-
soffashion.com/articles/intelligence/the-myth-of-made-in-
america-ttp-agreement.

Wainwright, Marcus. Rag & Bone. "A Message From Our Founder."
Accessed March 2020. https://www.rag-bone.com/from-our-
founder/.

CHAPTER 2

Edelkoort, Li. "The BoF Podcast: Li Edelkoort Says the Corona-
virus Is a Representation of our Conscience." March 27, 2020.
In *Special Edition Inside Fashion*. Produced by BOF TEAM.
Podcast, MP3 audio. https://www.businessoffashion.com/arti-
cles/podcasts/the-bof-podcast-li-edelkoort-on-how-covid-19-
is-ushering-in-the-age-of-the-amateur.

Reich, Charles A. The Greening of America. New York: Bantam,
1971.

CHAPTER 3

Papadopoulos, Mariah. "Veja's first line of running shoes is made
from rice waste, sugar cane and banana oil." *Fashion Journal*,
September 24, 2019. https://fashionjournal.com.au/fashion/
veja-making-morning-run-way-sustainable/.

Segran, Elizabeth. "Veja Wants To Make The Most Sustainable
Sneaker In The World." *Fast Company*, March 6, 2018. https://
www.fastcompany.com/40532184/veja-wants-to-make-the-
most-sustainable-sneaker-in-the-world.

CHAPTER 4

Lieber, Chavie. "The Fashion Rental Market Tested and Explained: Who Has the Best Service?." *Business of Fashion*, February 5, 2020. https://www.businessoffashion.com/articles/fashion-tech/fashion-rental-market-rent-the-runway-nuuly-letote-vince-unfold.

CHAPTER 5

CHAPTER 6

Binlot, Ann. "Vestiaire Collective Celebrates A Decade In Luxury Resale." *Forbes*, December 31, 2019.https://www.forbes.com/sites/abinlot/2020/12/31/vestiaire-collective-celebrates-a-decade-in-luxury-resale/#107e057976bc.

Vestiaire Collective. "The Smart Side of Fashion." Accessed June 2020.https://us.vestiairecollective.com/fashion-report/.

CHAPTER 7

Stella McCartney. "About Stella." Accessed March 19, 2020. https://www.stellamccartney.com/experience/en/about-stella/.

CHAPTER 8

CHAPTER 9

Cordero, Robert. "Li Edelkoort: 'Fashion is Old Fashioned' Trend forecaster Li Edelkoort presented key excerpts from her 'Anti-Fashion' Manifesto, challenging an industry she described as 'no longer part of the avant-garde'." *Business of*

Fashion, December 5, 2016.https://www.businessoffashion.
com/articles/voices/li-edelkoort-anti-fashion-manifesto-fash-
ion-is-old-fashioned.

Edelkoort, Lidewij. "Lidewij Edelkoort." Accessed March 20, 2020.
https://www.edelkoort.com/lidewij-edelkoort/.

CHAPTER 10

Alter, Charlotte, Suyin Haynes, and Justin Worland. "TIME 2019
Person of the Year." *TIME Magazine*, Dec. 23/Dec. 30 2019.
https://time.com/person-of-the-year-2019-greta-thunberg/.

CHAPTER 11

CHAPTER 12

Patagonia WornWear. "WornWear FAQ." Accessed November 25,
2019. https://wornwear.patagonia.com/faq.

TENCEL™. "TENCEL™ About." Accessed November 25, 2019.
https://www.tencel.com/about.

CONCLUSION

Maya, Singer." Can Fashion Be Political? Always- but now more
than ever. As the world undergoes a radical transformation,
Maya Singer looks at how the industry is reckoning with
momentous and much-needed change." *Vogue*, October 2020.

Wainwright, Marcus. Rag & Bone. "A Message From Our Founder."
Accessed March 2020. https://www.rag-bone.com/from-our-
founder/.

ACKNOWLEDGMENTS

- Martin & Jean Acquadro
- Chadwick Van Schoor
- Joyce Drolet
- Donna McCarthy
- John Beckey
- Steven Poe
- Janice Comeau
- David Sikora
- Alison Burns
- Savery Meurer
- Justin Baxter
- Lauren Acquadro
- Dawn Kemp
- DooRi Chung
- Joseph Kopp
- Lisa Baxter
- Steven Silvio
- Isabel Holden
- Olivia La Manna
- Brenda Sikora
- Steven-Alan Blyn Jacobs

- Joe Orlandella
- Jennifer White
- Grace Callahan
- Shelby Gale
- Nina Hsu
- Paul Crowley
- Heidi Sigourney
- Carolyn Holmes
- Mackenzie Madigan
- Tammy Donovan
- Joanne Demild
- Joanne Meurer
- Meg Meurer
- Jody O'Rourke
- Griffin Simonds
- Julia Fahey
- Morgan Powers
- Jolene Marangi
- Sonia Ikram
- Kellie LaPierre
- Jodi Connor
- Max De Jesus
- Jacqui Lajoie
- Susan Brosnahan
- Renee Lajoie
- Ellen Stockbridge
- Matt McCarthy
- Anne Yu
- Lauren Gisolfi
- Martha Soar
- Eleni S Nickolas
- Theresa A. Beretta

- Christopher Mitchell
- Lea Graham
- Savery Meurer
- Danielle Dumais
- Sarah Glass
- Theresa White
- Laura Hulme
- Sabrina Bergsten
- Matt Alexander
- Marni Dente
- Lily Caffrey-Levine
- Tim Hoang
- Laura Botelho
- Danny Jung
- Juliana Palmieri
- Eric Koester
- Megan Buckley
- Martha Villarreal
- Jay Sharma
- Shristhi Avasthi
- Kendall Baxter
- Olivia Galbraith
- Marina Melita
- Caroline Fahey
- Ana Mercurio-Pinto
- Kara LaPierre
- Evan Poe
- Leslie Frank
- Carolyn Rheinstein
- Ellen Iacopucci
- Katherine Burns
- Kristin Sikora

- Matt Pintea
- Olivia Allison
- Sophie-Anna Tamm
- Timothy Simpson
- Andrew Sottosanti
- Noelia Alvarenga

CPSIA information can be obtained
at www.ICGtesting.com
Printed in the USA
BVHW092354030121
596016BV00004BA/10